The Maritime Security Dilemma In The Gulf

Balancing Strait of Hormuz Protection with Regional Autonomy

GEW Reports & Analyses Team, Hichem Karoui (Ed.)

Global East-West (London)

Copyright © 2025 by GEW Reports & Analyses Team, Hichem Karoui (Editor)

Global East-West (London).

All rights reserved.

No portion of this book may be reproduced in any form without written permission from the publisher or author, except as permitted by copyright law.

Contents

1. Introduction to the Maritime Security Dilemma in the Strait of Hormuz — 1
2. Geopolitical Landscape of the Gulf Region — 13
3. Legal Frameworks Governing Maritime Security — 25
4. Strategic Military Capabilities and Deployments — 35
5. Threats to Maritime Security in the Strait of Hormuz — 47
6. Regional Autonomy and Sovereignty Concerns — 59
7. Economic Dimensions of Maritime Security — 71
8. Diplomatic Strategies and Multilateral Engagements — 81
9. Technological Innovations and Maritime Domain Awareness — 93
10. Crisis Management and Conflict Resolution Mechanisms — 103
11. Building Regional Security Architectures — 115
12. Practical Strategies for Balancing Security and Autonomy — 127

13.	Future Trends and Emerging Challenges	141
14.	Policy Recommendations and Implementation Frameworks	153
15.	Conclusion and Path Forward	165
References		179

1
Introduction to the Maritime Security Dilemma in the Strait of Hormuz

Historical Significance and Strategic Importance of the Strait of Hormuz

The Strait of Hormuz has served for centuries as an indispensable maritime corridor, shaping both regional trade and the evolution of interstate relations. Functionally, the passage has always represented the point of intersection for the East-West trade axis, allowing merchants and envoys to traverse the narrow waters and establish linkages prized for both commercial and cultural value. The concourse of caravans and later maritime traffic not only allowed commodities to flow but also transmitted religious, artistic, and linguistic influences, weaving an interlinked fabric of shared heritage among the littoral states. The contest for supervisory authority over the Strait has repeatedly reframed the fortunes of rising and waning imperial actors, rendering the waterway both an economic asset and a theatre of war. Successive contests—often asymmetrical—attest that the Strait was seldom rendered peripheral, but remained a geographical hinge upon which dynastic stability turned.

Conjectural threats, whether from intra-regional rivalry, weather-induced navigational hazards, or endemic piracy, led coastal and supervenient states alike to maintain, on a judicious and sometimes aggressive footing, a persistent international maritime security presence designed to uphold the passage's reliability and, by extension, to manage the power geometry the Strait perpetually reproduced. These security measures illustrate the architectonic character of the Strait, revealing its dual function as both commercial corridor and theatre of military-diplomatic calculus. Ever-shifting constellations of alliances and rivalries among the Gulf states reshape the region's geopolitical landscape, with the Strait of Hormuz serving as a perpetual focal point. The vast hydrocarbon find in the Gulf recalibrated the Strait's relative value on this board, elevating its salience in contemporary international politics.

The Strait has therefore achieved canonical status as one of the world's preeminent energy choke points. Roughly one-fifth of global hydrocarbon export capacity transits these constricted waters, positioning the thoroughfare as an indispensable physiognomy of planetary energy security. This stance has solicited the vigilant gaze of principal state and commercial actors, both consumers and producers, who view custodial influence here as an imperative of strategic fortification. Consequent developments along the strait project authority well beyond its aqueous periphery. Modifications of accessibility or of security atmosphere within the corridor register as immediate price signals—permissive suppertime, futures easement, for instance—which propagate upward and outward into transoceanic energy markets. Softer price effects design export revenues, import bilaterals, risk premiums, and even the composite fragility of states and of private actors dependent on oil returns. Within this anticipatory register, stakeholders find it imperative to calibrate forecast models to the corridor, accounting for its iterative redefinition as a principal energy frontier.

Defining the Maritime Security Dilemma: Concepts and Scope

Maritime security encompasses the protection of national interests in coastal and offshore environments from a range of threats, including piracy and illicit trafficking, contested waters, and the risk of overt military conflict. It encompasses the safeguarding of critical maritime arteries, hydrocarbon deposits, and maritime critical infrastructure, ultimately ensuring the unobstructed transit of commodities and the maintenance of national and regional security. The maritime security calculus is particularly vivid in the case of the Strait of Hormuz, a narrow and yet strategically vital corridor through which a substantial proportion of the global hydrocarbon market passes. The Strait constitutes the principal westward outlet of the Persian Gulf, linking it to the Arabian Sea and thereby functioning as a connecting theatre of regional influence and international trade. This geographical corridor thus becomes the inevitable centre of attention in security deliberations of the Gulf Cooperation Council members, as well as of extra-regional actors whose strategic and economic interests extend into the Arabian Peninsula. Maritime security in this context, however, is not limited strictly to military confrontation and asymmetric campaigns, but increasingly is framed by interdependencies, hybrid risks, and the protection of critical non-state actors.

The contemporary understanding of maritime security in the Gulf encompasses a triad of threats: terrorism, environmental degradation, and the protection of critical undersea infrastructure, including hydrocarbon pipelines and global communication cables. Because the region is a principal artery of the world's energy trade, any maritime insecurity can rapidly translate local disruptions into elevated risk premiums, volatility in energy markets, and subsequent ripple effects that jeopardise both state and corporate balance sheets. This intricate web of dependency elevates the maritime security calculus beyond the confines of territorial jurisdictions, compelling a regime that effectively blends sustained national stewardship with continual participative diplomacy among both regional and extra-regional actors. Coastal states in the Gulf routinely engage in sophisticated balancing, asserting sovereign jurisdiction while concurrently providing the navigational assurances that international law and the global trading system prescribe. Grasping Gulf maritime security, therefore, requires an appreciation of overlapping, competing mandates—protection of security infrastructures, stewardship of biologically and economically vital coastal and maritime ecosystems, and apparent state legitimacy through navigational sovereignty. Thus, maritime security is effectively the management of rapidly evolving complex risk environments, where the interplay of national and global interest may afford control of maritime decision points that nonetheless evolve into enduring instruments of economic statecraft and geopolitical leverage.

The strategic environment within the Strait of Hormuz is exacerbated by its constricted waters. This geographic constraint magnifies the operational and political significance of the corridor for any maritime actor. Calculations conducted by Gulf governments and external powers alike must incorporate not only imminent threats—kinetic or hybrid—but also the manifold and interdependent functions that the waterway performs, including the transport of hydrocarbons, projection of naval capabilities, and, indirectly, the conduct of diplomacy. Maintenance of such a holistic perspective reveals the systematic interdependence of Gulf security and the wider balances performed by contemporary consensus mechanisms. It therefore represents a necessary preparatory step for any policy discourse addressing the security dilemmas confronting the peninsula states and their global partners.

The security dilemma confronting the Arabian Gulf maritime environment is produced by the tight interlacing of rival sovereignty claims, foreign military engagements, and emergent hybrid threats, all catalysed by globalised energy interdependence. Stability consequently hinges on the orchestration of irreducibly contradictory policy vectors: the emphatic assertion of territorial sovereignty by regional states, the equally adamant exercise of the right of innocent passage by the wider maritime community, and the parallel, if fragmentary, deployment of rules of Customary International Law, including the United Nations Convention on the Law of the Sea. For the Khaleej (Gulf) states, therefore, the forward basing or episodic forward deployment of naval contingents is a manifest heir to domestic economies of resolve, designed overtly to project both deterrent credibility and command of the littoral and its Exclusive Economic Zone, yet implicitly signalling to all rival naval manifestations that maritime sovereignty still constitutes a valid operational and jurisdictional currency, even through the deterrent prism of proportional, if not counter-productive, force.

Simultaneously, a pronounced global imperative to keep vital maritime routes free from disruption has prompted the deployment of navy forces from outside the region, including those of the United States, Europe, and various Asian states.

This external presence intersects inseparably with the protective measures pursued by the littoral states, individually and collectively, thereby producing a fragile equilibrium in which procedural steps adopted by any single power for defensive purposes may be perceived as menacing by others, thereby catalysing an enduring cycle of distrust and imitative rivalry.

The maritime dimension of this security dilemma cannot be neatly detached from the wider polarisation between the aspired regional equilibrium and the reach of international security structures. On the one hand, the Gulf Cooperation Council states defend their sovereign prerogative to regulate all operations in their territorial and adjacent waters, frequently receiving or rejecting overt manifestations of foreign maritime power with impatience bordering on hostility. Conversely, established legal norms, principally those incorporated in the United Nations Convention on the Law of the Sea, cast free navigation and the doctrine of innocent passage as collective entitlements. The juxtaposition of these necessitous and at times antithetical objectives obliges all parties to engage in sustained, and often painstaking, negotiation accompanied by disciplined, unequivocal signalling and messaging practice, lest ambiguous actions precipitate militarised, unintended escalation.

Military exercises or maritime patrol campaigns in the Strait of Hormuz, for instance, may be regarded as prudent defence or as provocatively muscular, the label hinging entirely on the viewer's vantage. Such dual readings illustrate that security calculations can no longer be confined to conventional military terms. Maritime security in the Gulf, therefore, extends to safeguarding production and consumption nodes along the Sea Lines of Communication, to managing the sustained and migratory pressures on regional fish stocks, and to positioning rapid-onset plans in the wake of hydrocarbon-related spills or mineral-carrier groundings. States of the Gulf, while formulating defence projects, must measure rising national project timelines against both the choreography of foreland naval deployments and the operational burdens revealed by global dependency on still-accruing supply routes. Non-state maritime headaches, be they the trending density of diesel-band piracy or the recombinant, often transient, smuggling and diversionary overlays, prescribe compounded and layered responses.

These responses, articulating naval dissuasive heft, governed space through enforceable directives and corridor advisory sharing, placing a premium on regional pools of collective calculation. Yet, such cooperative inclinations, whether codified through cooperative structures or tethered through tacit understanding, are consistently weighed down by the gravitational forces of diverging national priorities and by the in-built redistributions of confidence that fluctuate through repeated interaction. When addressing the enduring security dilemma in the Gulf maritime littoral, decision-makers face the imperative of cultivating enduring levels of confidence and designing mechanisms that, while fortifying collective security objectives, dampen the drumbeat of ever-ascendant hazard. It is thus through mechanisms of regional aggregation, most notably the Gulf Cooperation Council (GCC), and through calibrated engagement with wider multinational security architectures, that Gulf littoral states now operationalise the trade-off between explicit claims of sovereignty and the more indirect, though predominant, utility of durable stability.

A nuanced understanding of divergent yet overlapping

hierarchies of interest, coupled with the necessary acknowledgement of the various logics that animate each coastal capital, is indispensable to the calibrated governance of the Strait of Hormuz and the maritime environment more broadly. One operational modality that continues to yield value involves the deliberate engineering of transparency and dialogue between the different operational forces, whether naval or aerial, that now routinely work in these waters. Precise confidence-building ratios – including periodic and bilaterally observed exercises, the upfront and routine sharing of maritime movement updates, and affiliate channels, arguably linked to respective national operations centres – have in the past demonstrated that the thresholds of evasive or miscalculated engagement can be successfully recalibrated. A reciprocal emphasis upon multinational, combined responses to non-combat contingencies, such as routine piracy, or equally pressing but non-security emergencies, such as oil-platform distress, not only expands an infrastructure of cooperation but distributes those dividends into the wider regional harmonisation tableau. Thus, stakeholders can progressively reorder the prevailing multiplicity of claims and imperatives around the anchor of an emergent, if nascent, collective intent.

Objectives and Scope of the Book: Balancing Security and Regional Autonomy

The Strait of Hormuz remains an irreplaceable corridor for global hydrocarbons and merchandise, thereby attracting both concentrated diplomatic mediation and persistent security apprehension. This volume aims to outline the complex challenges facing Gulf states and their neighbouring polities as they balance the demands of maritime security, territorial integrity, and sustained economic stability. In pursuing this objective, the text systematically examines the core variables that determine the interplay between defensive postures and the resolute intention of states to maintain supremacy over national waters and marine resources. Against this analytical backdrop, the study seeks axiomatic consideration of configurations that ascertain maritime safety, yet incrementally attenuate pressures that might otherwise encroach upon expressive geographic autonomy.

Conclusively, the volume underlines the pre-eminent value Gulf polities attribute to self-governance and, conversely, their wary disposition toward transregional official and extra-regional non-official stakeholders whose involvement could jeopardise the institutional prerogatives of statehood. This investigation assesses multiple maritime security initiatives—fleet presence, cooperative code-of-conduct pacts, and multilateral confidence-building workshops—evaluating their capacity for implementation while maintaining strict respect for sovereign prerogatives. The exposition underscores mechanisms through which observable deterrent, interdiction, and maritime-domain awareness objectives may be satisfactorily attained without encroaching upon local jurisdiction, thereby cultivating the political currency of mutual reassurance among littoral states, enhancing the security of critical waterborne supply chains, and avoiding the corrosive consequences of perceived encroachment upon state autonomy or collective historical narratives.

Underlying the empirical inquiry, the study situates current initiatives within a historical continuum of regional security evolution, examining the intersection of emergent hinterland cartographies, transnational commercial dependencies, and evolving security architectures in the Gulf. It systematically interrogates the strategic orientations and operational designs of neighbouring heavyweights—Saudi Arabia, Iran, the United Arab Emirates, and Oman—alongside extra-regional influents, notably the United States, China, and the European Union, interrogating the mechanisms through which each actor contributes to or recalibrates the security milieu, weighing the exportation of deterrent capability against regional legislative autonomy and systemic stability.

The study likewise highlights persistent regional vulnerabilities—piracy, drug and weapon smuggling, and the low-level, permanent military posturing—together with larger transboundary dynamics, most critically climate change and the uneven distribution, extraction, and contestation of energy and fresh-water resources, all of which conspire to strain the maritime safety of the Hormuz corridor. By integrating these diverse pressures into a single analytical framework, the document illustrates the dialectical ways in which both endogenous and exogenous actors condition the formulation of security protocols, and recommends that stability be architected in a manner that neither entrusts maritime routes to foreign tutelage nor transfers excessive state power that might compromise local legitimacy. Contemporary policy and academic actors are advised to situate all hazard analysis and response within the broader dialectic of politics, development, and cultural identity that characterises the maritime domain.

A meritocratic and persistent safety architecture in Hormuz can only be scaffolded by continuously recalibrating maritime policy against the interlaced universe of local and extra-local trade dynamics, energy interdependence, migratory labour patterns, and the gestural politics of identity. The study, therefore, places a premium not so much on harder security commodities—such as naval assets and patrols—executed in isolation, but on the leads and reciprocal give-and-take generated by low-visibility, low-risk, and structurally bi-level diplomatic conversations. Regional prudence recommends, moreover, the endorsement of a noticeably distributive safety architecture, that is, the embedding of local power layers in surveillance, monitoring, and port management, whereby both national and extra-national assets are allowed to apportion protection and inspection responsibilities so that no single national or alliance prism is allowed to monopolise the corridor's informational and enforcement architecture.

2
Geopolitical Landscape of the Gulf Region

The Strait of Hormuz, a vital waterway connecting the Persian Gulf to the Gulf of Oman, experiences intense maritime traffic, making its security a paramount concern. As a result, regional nations have forged various maritime agreements aimed at curbing piracy, smuggling, and other maritime crimes (Islam MS, 2024). The Gulf Cooperation Council (GCC), for instance, has developed maritime protocols aimed at promoting cooperation among its member states. Information sharing and joint patrols are key elements of these protocols, aimed at enhancing maritime security in the Gulf, in general. These protocols provide a legal framework for navies and coast guards to coordinate their efforts, ensuring the safe passage of goods and energy resources, although compliance varies.

One notable regional effort is the Djibouti Code of Conduct (DCoC). Initially focused on piracy off the coast of Somalia, its scope has broadened to encompass wider maritime threats, involving participating Gulf states. This expansion generally strengthens regional cooperation. The DCoC outlines guidelines for information sharing, coordinated naval operations, and capacity building. By emphasising transparency and trust, it seeks to foster regional ownership of maritime security.

The practical impact of the DCoC includes a decrease in piracy incidents and illegal maritime activities in the Gulf, which can be attributed to enhanced monitoring and joint exercises. Both GCC protocols and the Djibouti Code of Conduct aim to create a common front against maritime challenges, reducing tensions and securing navigation in the Strait of Hormuz. While the GCC primarily involves six Gulf states with shared economic and political interests, the DCoC includes a broader range of regional partners, like East African nations. These agreements include specific legal provisions regarding interdiction, offender handling, and respect for sovereignty, striking a balance between effective collective action and national interests. Harmonising these regional maritime agreements is complicated. States want to maintain sovereignty over their waters and security, with Persian Gulf nations wary of external interference and protective of their autonomy (Islam MS, 2024). This can limit the depth of cooperation or slow the implementation of shared protocols. Varying naval capabilities and enforcement capacities among states also affect compliance; some members may be less equipped to monitor and respond effectively, potentially creating security gaps (Islam MS, 2024).

The United Nations Convention on the Law of the Sea (UNCLOS) plays a critical role, offering a widely accepted international legal framework that complements regional agreements. UNCLOS defines rights and responsibilities related to territorial seas, exclusive economic zones, and freedom of navigation, though interpretations vary (Islam MS, 2024). Regional agreements often align with UNCLOS to enhance legitimacy and ensure security arrangements comply with international law. However, differing interpretations regarding military passage or naval exercises can sometimes create friction. Despite these challenges, opportunities exist to strengthen cooperation by enhancing legal harmonisation and mutual trust. Mechanisms for dispute resolution and joint training can promote compliance and build confidence. Coordination efforts that respect sovereignty while encouraging information sharing and timely responses have improved. Expanding technical cooperation and investing in maritime domain awareness technologies can also bridge resource gaps. By focusing on shared interests, such as protecting energy exports and maintaining open shipping lanes, regional actors can work towards more coherent frameworks that balance national interests and collective security. For policymakers and diplomats, focusing on transparent communication and incremental trust-building is crucial. Investing in joint maritime exercises and combined operational centres where real-time information is exchanged can foster collaboration without threatening sovereignty. Engaging with UNCLOS experts ensures regional practices are grounded in international law, reducing the risk of misunderstandings (Islam MS, 2024).

Key Regional Actors and Their Strategic Interests

The Strait of Hormuz, a relatively narrow waterway, plays a crucial role in the broader context of global maritime security. Arguably the world's most vital chokepoint, a large proportion of the world's oil traverses this strategic strait. For Gulf nation-states, notably Saudi Arabia, Kuwait, and the United Arab Emirates, the safety and security of this passage are of paramount importance (Brewster et al., 2014). Control here not only underpins economic security—it also bolsters political sway within global energy markets. Major oil producers depend on the strait to export their crude; thus, its security is naturally a primary concern. Military conflict or regional political instability could lead to skyrocketing oil prices with potential global economic repercussions. As such, Gulf stakeholders find themselves heavily invested in sustaining a stable navigation environment throughout these waters. The interests of external powers, which refer to countries or entities outside the Gulf region, also significantly come into play. The United States, for example, maintains a longstanding military presence in the region, primarily aimed at protecting shipping routes from threats posed by regional actors, such as Iran (Faculty of the Department of Affairs NS et al., 1998). Maintaining energy security for both Europe and China depends on ensuring unhindered access to oil. Economic interests align with strategic calculations, leading these foreign powers to engage in diplomatic and, sometimes, military engagements to ensure the strait remains accessible and guarded against threats. These complex relationships within this maritime space illustrate the delicate balancing act required of all involved, from Gulf countries to global powers, each holding a significant stake in the Strait of Hormuz.

On the other hand, the Gulf Cooperation Council (GCC) nations—Saudi Arabia and the UAE, notably—tend to prioritise cooperation with external powers, looking to counterbalance Iran's assertiveness. The GCC has invested considerably in collective security arrangements, depending on alliances with countries like the United States to safeguard the Strait of Hormuz. Contractual agreements that provide military support, plus strategic partnerships, are pivotal in bolstering their security. Diplomatically, these Gulf states often pursue pathways to mitigate threats and foster stability through economic partnerships and multilateral talks. However, this approach presents challenges in most cases. For example, internal divisions within the GCC, such as differing views on regional policies or security strategies, can impede cohesive security responses. Even with external powers (the United States and European countries) maintaining a significant presence in the region, ensuring security in the Strait of Hormuz remains multifaceted. The external interests, it seems, often reflect economic dependencies while avoiding deeper entanglement in regional disputes. This situation sometimes leads to tensions, particularly when overseas military forces focus on simply deterring threats, rather than resolving underlying conflicts. In this intricate matrix of interests, a variety of actors navigate their strategies, always aware of any changes that may occur.

Table (1): Key Regional Actors and Their Strategic Interests in the Strait of Hormuz

Country	Strategic Interest
Iran	Control over the Strait to secure oil exports and regional influence
Saudi Arabia	Ensuring free passage for oil exports and regional stability
United Arab Emirates	Maintaining secure maritime routes for trade and energy exports
Oman	Preserving neutral maritime routes and regional peace
Qatar	Safeguarding LNG exports and regional security

Historical Evolution of Gulf Security Dynamics

The Gulf's security has historically been defined by its geography and trade routes, with the Strait of Hormuz serving as a crucial chokepoint for global energy (Gama IDA et al., 2021). This narrow passage, connecting the Arabian Gulf with the Gulf of Oman and the Arabian Sea, has made controlling it a matter of strategic importance. Empires and trading powers, since ancient times, have viewed the Gulf as more than just a source of wealth; it is a corridor whose security is often determined by maritime dominance. The 20th century saw the importance of this waterway amplified by the discovery of extensive oil reserves, which drew international attention and complicated the security concerns in the Gulf. Initially, European imperial powers, such as the British Empire, were primarily interested in protecting maritime routes and oil supplies; their influence was exerted through protectorate arrangements rather than direct territorial control (Gama IDA et al., 2021).

During the Cold War, the Strait of Hormuz gained even greater strategic importance, resulting in increased military involvement by external powers. Local politics, tribal affiliations, and regional rivalries would consistently interact with these external elements to shape a complex security situation. In the latter half of the 20th century, a balance, often uneasy, existed between local sovereignty efforts and the presence of foreign military forces.

The emergence of Saudi Arabia, the United Arab Emirates, Qatar, Kuwait, and other Gulf states introduced new actors seeking to address threats from both inside and outside. While a regional desire for autonomy persisted, external powers, primarily the United States and the United Kingdom, were often invited to provide security guarantees. Key moments, such as the Iranian Revolution (1979) and the Iran-Iraq War, caused shifts in this balance by adding regional tensions and strategic complexity.

These events revealed how local conflicts could become entwined with broader geopolitical competition. The Gulf War (1990-1991) represents a crucial moment regarding the international role in Gulf security, leading to a U.S.-led coalition intervening to remove Iraqi forces from Kuwait. This intervention set a precedent for future arrangements, while also underscoring the limits of regional capabilities and highlighting the need to understand Gulf dynamics in relation to global strategies (Bergeron JH, 2021). The Gulf's security is a result of different competing variables, and the region's continuous value to the global economy means that its stability will remain a point of concern.

Table (2): Historical Evolution of Gulf Security Dynamics

Year	Event
1980	Iran-Iraq War begins, leading to significant regional instability.
1990	Iraq's invasion of Kuwait prompts the Gulf Cooperation Council (GCC) to seek external military assistance.
2003	U.S. invasion of Iraq further alters regional security dynamics.
2011	Arab Spring uprisings influence political landscapes in Gulf states.
2014	Emergence of ISIS challenges regional security and prompts GCC responses.
2017	Publication of 'The Changing Security Dynamics of the Persian Gulf' examines evolving security threats.

External Powers and Their Influence in the Strait of Hormuz

The Gulf's security landscape is undeniably shaped by external involvement. For example, recent U.S. naval deployments in the Gulf, along with joint drills conducted with Gulf Cooperation Council (GCC) members, reflect ongoing attempts to foster stability within a notably complex and volatile area (Faculty of the Department of Affairs NS et al., 1998). However, regional tensions, notably the Saudi-Iranian rivalry, continue to influence threat perceptions and fuel proxy wars, which are conflicts where external powers support opposing sides, adding layers to the security picture. These proxy wars often involve non-state actors and can be fuelled by ideological, political, or economic interests. For Gulf states, a core challenge is how to preserve their sovereignty while collaborating on security matters with influential allies; it is about balancing outside influences alongside addressing pressing domestic political and economic issues. Comprehending this changing balance requires examining the Gulf's past experiences with colonialism, independence, and conflict, as well as the interests of outside powers, whose naval and military presence have often been a defining aspect of the region's security arrangements. Gulf nations have been increasing their investments in their own defence sectors and enhancing military strength, aiming to reduce vulnerabilities and ensure that foreign alliances align with national interests. Looking forward, Gulf security is likely to continue being shaped by shifting alliances, economic ties, and strategic risks, and control over the Strait of Hormuz is likely to remain a pivotal element in the region's stability and global importance.

The Strait of Hormuz, a narrow channel connecting the Persian Gulf to the wider Gulf of Oman, serves as a crucial artery for global oil transportation (Manfred Häfner et al., 2023). Unsurprisingly, its significance has drawn the attention of numerous external powers, each with its own agenda. The U.S. has historically been a key player in the region, perceiving the Strait as essential for upholding global energy security and ensuring the freedom of navigation. American naval forces frequently patrol here, aiming to deter disruptions and demonstrate their strength, thereby showing a commitment to stability and trade (Selth A, 2022).

In addition to this, the U.S. keeps military installations in the area, assisting allies and watching Iran, plus other regional entities. This effectively grants Washington considerable sway over maritime security, preserving Western interests internationally. China, with its growing energy needs, also has significant stakes. Beijing views the Strait of Hormuz as a crucial route for its oil; in fact, over a third of its imports come this way. China tends to invest in infrastructure and use diplomacy with Gulf nations, securing energy routes without direct military action. Naval visits and port calls demonstrate a desire to safeguard economic interests while avoiding direct conflict. This shows a well-rounded approach of economic ties alongside military and diplomatic actions, somewhat challenging traditional Western influence. Regional players—Iran, Saudi Arabia, the UAE, and Oman—are also critical in moulding the area's geopolitics. Iran, especially, views the Strait as a trump card and will occasionally threaten closure to bargain with other nations. Their naval patrols are common, and they have developed tactics such as using mines and drones, which are uncrewed aerial vehicles, to contest outside power. These tactics are part of Iran's asymmetric warfare strategy, which aims to counter the technological superiority of its adversaries. This has fuelled tension and fostered a complex security situation indicative of regional power dynamics.

Gulf Security Dynamics

Gulf Cooperation Council (GCC) states, such as Saudi Arabia and the UAE, have established strategic alliances with Western nations, particularly the United States. This aims to enhance their security and counter Iran's regional ambitions (Islam MS, 2024). Oman, however, often mediates due to its geography and desire for stability, while maintaining good relations with Iran. This all adds complexity to the influence of external powers, making the Strait a contested area. It is not just military and economic; diplomatic initiatives and alliances matter too. The US has established partnerships through military aid, intelligence sharing, and exercises, thereby creating a security "umbrella" (Sahakyan, 2024).

China's Belt and Road Initiative (BRI) includes investments that enhance energy access, fostering a strategic balance that aligns with economic objectives. Iran's tactics generally aim to weaken Western dominance by controlling the Strait of Hormuz. As these powers pursue their interests, their actions intersect or conflict, which can heighten tensions. This makes the Strait's control a global concern, influencing international policies. External interventions deeply affect Gulf countries' sovereignty. The free operation of outside powers can limit the ability of regional governments to make independent security decisions. Foreign patrols or blockades, even for international interests, might be seen as infringements.

Table (3): Gulf Cooperation Council (GCC) Defence Expenditures and U.S. Military Sales (2007-2010)

Year	GCC Defense Expenditure (USD Billion)	U.S. Military Sales to GCC (USD Billion)
2007	25	5
2008	27.5	6
2009	30	7
2010	32.5	8

Gulf states face a delicate balance: they must manage Western partnerships while maintaining cooperation with neighbours like Iran and Oman. The presence of external actors further complicates regional security, sometimes leading to proxy conflicts. External powers attempt to shape the regional order to their favour, potentially harming local stability. Gulf security is closely tied to the actions of these external powers. Interventions, such as naval exercises or arms sales, can affect regional stability, potentially deterring threats but also provoking escalation. US patrols aim for safe passage, but they can provoke Iranian responses, such as interception. China's growing naval presence is regarded with caution by Gulf states, which generally prefer a balance of engagement and restraint. This web raises the likelihood of miscalculations escalating into wider conflicts. Thus, stability depends on sustained dialogue and the ability of regional actors to manage external pressures, safeguarding their interests.

3
Legal Frameworks Governing Maritime Security

This chapter examines the legal frameworks relevant to maritime security, exploring how international law, regional treaties, and national regulations interact to influence maritime security operations in the Strait of Hormuz. This strategically important maritime area, crucial for global oil transportation, presents specific legal challenges as countries strive to balance protecting their own interests and respecting the autonomy of regional participants. While the United Nations Convention on the Law of the Sea (UNCLOS) provides a fundamental legal structure, outlining the rights and responsibilities of states in maritime areas, its application can be disputed when national security priorities clash (Islam MS, 2024). Moreover, the evolving characteristics of maritime threats, such as piracy and aggression from state actors, necessitate that these legal frameworks adapt to meet current challenges. The growing role of non-state actors and the introduction of new technologies in maritime activities add complexity to the legal environment, requiring a strong response from international legal bodies and regional collaborations (Sahakyan M, 2024). A complete grasp of these legal mechanisms is essential for policymakers. It informs strategies for securing maritime routes while also encouraging regional stability and cooperation. It is also vital in ensuring the rights of neighbouring states are respected, even amidst global maritime pressures.

International Maritime Law and the Strait of Hormuz (UNCLOS and Others)

UNCLOS, or the United Nations Convention on the Law of the Sea, serves as a foundational framework for understanding maritime law. It addresses many things concerning the oceans. Adopted in 1982, UNCLOS (Aldawish et al., 2025) outlines the rights and responsibilities of coastal countries, provides guidance on navigating international waters, and seeks to strike a balance between competing national interests while promoting peaceful interactions at sea. Straits, for example, such as the Strait of Hormuz, are important geostrategic choke points that illustrate the complexity of these maritime claims. Roughly a fifth of the world's oil trade passes through this region each year (Aldawish et al., 2025), highlighting the risk of conflict in areas where different states make conflicting claims on maritime territory. The United States also plays a role, pushing for adherence to UNCLOS through its Freedom of Navigation Program, which carries out naval operations intended to challenge maritime claims that the U.S. views as inconsistent with international law. Understanding how these legal frameworks govern passage through contested areas and reflect broader geopolitical strategies is increasingly important as maritime navigation evolves. This broad view highlights the complex relationships between law, national security, and international trade, underscoring the vital need for robust legal tools to mitigate conflict and foster stability in the world's oceans.

Navigating the complexities of territorial waters involves grappling with critical issues such as fishing rights and the extraction of mineral resources. The Strait of Hormuz, a narrow passage between Oman and Iran, is a vital artery —a key maritime choke point that sees a large percentage of the world's oil pass through its waters. Coastal nations, as per the United Nations Convention on the Law of the Sea (UNCLOS), exercise sovereignty over their territorial waters, generally extending up to 12 nautical miles from their baseline. This has, naturally, substantial implications for both maritime traffic and regional security (Karim A et al., 2023). Beyond UNCLOS, several other international legal documents and accepted customary practices impact the maritime security situation, specifically in the Strait of Hormuz.

The International Maritime Organisation (IMO) plays a crucial role in regulating international shipping practices and, of course, in ensuring safety at sea, especially in areas considered high-risk, such as this very strait. A wide range of resolutions and guidelines, developed by the IMO, focus on environmental protection and navigational safety. These are paramount, really, to preventing maritime accidents and potential pollution incidents (Islam MS, 2024). Bilateral and multilateral treaties among Gulf states also significantly shape the maritime security environment. One can consider, for instance, the 2004 Agreement on Maritime Security Cooperation between Iran and Oman, which establishes important protocols for vessels operating in this very strategic zone. These agreements, however, often encounter limitations due to the intricate geopolitical factors at play, characterised by rivalries and ever-shifting alliances among the various regional powers.

Customary international law also has a noticeable influence in the maritime domain, particularly in how states behave in accordance with established maritime norms. Despite these challenges, regional countries might seek to enhance their autonomy concerning maritime policies. This could potentially lead to the development of innovative approaches for achieving collective security. Think about joint military drills, for example, or perhaps security dialogues, both of which could foster cooperation while addressing shared maritime threats. Effectively addressing persistent concerns, such as piracy, smuggling, or other illegal activities in the Strait, requires collaboration, as no single nation can manage these challenges alone. Consequently, a solid understanding of the current legal frameworks, coupled with fostering strong regional partnerships, becomes a crucial component in the broader effort to maintain both security and overall stability within this vitally important maritime corridor.

Regional Maritime Agreements and Their Effectiveness

The Strait of Hormuz, a crucial global waterway connecting the Persian Gulf to the Gulf of Oman (Faculty of the Department of Affairs NS et al., 1998), sees substantial maritime traffic. Protecting its security has prompted regional nations to forge maritime agreements targeting piracy, smuggling, and other maritime crimes. The Gulf Cooperation Council (GCC) has established several maritime protocols focused on cooperation, information sharing, and joint patrols to enhance security in the Gulf (Ostrom et al., 2021). These protocols offer a legal basis for navies and coast guards to coordinate their efforts, securing the flow of resources. One prominent initiative is the Djibouti Code of Conduct (DCoC).

While it initially addressed counter-piracy off Somalia, it has grown to include broader maritime threats relevant to participating Gulf states. The DCoC sets guidelines for information sharing and coordinated operations; its legal provisions emphasise regional ownership, building trust via transparent practices. We've seen its impact in reduced piracy incidents due to improved monitoring. Both the GCC protocols and the DCoC aim to create a unified approach, reducing tensions in the Strait of Hormuz. The GCC mainly involves six member states with shared interests, while the DCoC ropes in other partners, providing a broader framework.

These agreements have legal stipulations on interdiction and offender handling, balancing sovereignty with the need for collective action. Such legal clarity helps reduce potential misunderstandings that could arise from unilateral actions. However, harmonising these agreements faces challenges, especially concerning sovereignty over territorial waters. Nations are wary of interference and prefer autonomy in decision-making. This concern can sometimes limit cooperation or slow the adoption of protocols.

Furthermore, differing naval capabilities impact compliance; some members may lack the resources to monitor effectively, creating security gaps. The United Nations Convention on the Law of the Sea (UNCLOS) provides a widely accepted legal framework that often complements regional agreements. UNCLOS defines rights related to territorial seas and navigation, recognised by Gulf states. Regional agreements align with UNCLOS to ensure legitimacy, but different interpretations regarding military passage sometimes cause friction. Despite these challenges, there are avenues to strengthen cooperation through legal harmonisation and trust-building. Dispute resolution mechanisms and joint training can promote compliance. Coordination that respects sovereignty while encouraging information sharing has improved. Expanding technical cooperation can also bridge resource gaps. By focusing on shared interests, such as energy exports, regional actors can strive for more coherent frameworks that balance national and collective safety.

Table (4): Effectiveness of Regional Maritime Agreements in Combating Illegal, unreported, and unregulated (IUU) Fishing

Agreement	Year Enacted	Purpose	Impact
Port State Measures Agreement (PSMA)	2016	Prevent, deter, and eliminate illegal, unreported, and unregulated (IUU) fishing by implementing effective port state measures.	Enhances global capacity to detect IUU fishing and prevents illegally caught fish from entering international markets.
Western and Central Pacific Fisheries Commission (WCPFC)	2004	Manage fisheries resources beyond areas of national jurisdiction in the Western and Central Pacific Ocean.	Developed a fully developed boarding and inspection protocol for high seas enforcement, leading to improved governance and cooperation for long-term resource management.
Regional Port State Control Memorandums of Understanding (MOU)	Various (e.g., Paris MOU in 1982, Tokyo MOU in 1993)	Enhance enforcement of marine pollution and vessel safety laws against visiting vessels through regional cooperation.	Aims to prevent the operation of substandard ships and avoid distorting competition between ports by ensuring uniform application of standards.

Legal Challenges in Enforcing Maritime Sovereignty and Security

Interruptions to traffic in the Strait of Hormuz can lead to significant fluctuations in global oil prices, resulting in impacts across energy markets, as recent analyses have highlighted (Kumara et al., 2021). For Gulf economies, which rely heavily on maritime trade, such disruptions pose a significant threat to economic stability and investor confidence, as oil exports are crucial. Furthermore, international shipping companies may encounter higher insurance rates, additional rerouting costs, and operational delays, as noted in various studies. Non-state actor activities complicate the security landscape and challenge the sovereignty of coastal states. Researchers have examined the interaction between state power and non-state influences in maritime contexts. Such interventions often reflect broader regional tensions, with backing from external powers seeking to project influence, posing challenges to local governance. This requires a keen understanding from policymakers and scholars focused on Gulf security and international maritime governance.

Gulf states have addressed these challenges through military presence, legal reforms, and enhanced surveillance, per regional initiatives (Shaheen et al., 2025). The United Arab Emirates, Saudi Arabia, and Oman have invested in coastal defences and naval capabilities to monitor and control their territorial waters, showing a more proactive security stance. They conduct joint exercises to improve coordination and share intelligence on maritime activities, indicating a collaborative approach to regional security matters. International partners, including the United States, the United Kingdom, and coalition forces, support these efforts by maintaining a naval presence to protect global shipping lanes and reinforcing collective security. Yet, these operations require careful balancing between deterring threats and avoiding actions that might escalate tensions, necessitating careful diplomatic handling. Diplomatic initiatives are also crucial for striking a balance between security and regional autonomy, emphasising the importance of multilateral negotiations.

Gulf Cooperation Council (GCC) members operate within international frameworks, such as the International Maritime Organisation, and adhere to United Nations conventions to assert their rights while promoting cooperative security. This strategy emphasises the importance of legal and institutional frameworks. Some Gulf states have sought to create specialised maritime task forces for sharing real-time intelligence, addressing piracy and smuggling without escalating confrontation. These approaches reflect the sensitivity of the strait's geopolitical position—too much external meddling risks undermining the sovereignty of Gulf nations, whereas insufficient collaboration leaves critical vulnerabilities unaddressed. International actors also recognise the need to support Gulf efforts. This involves capacity-building for coast guards, technology transfers for surveillance, and coordination with commercial shipping to enhance threat awareness, all of which point to synergy between state and non-state actors. Diplomats and experts emphasise the importance of maintaining open communication, even between adversaries, to reduce misunderstandings and prevent escalations, which is crucial in the region.

Additionally, some Gulf countries occasionally engage in dialogue with neighbouring non-state actors when practical, addressing causes such as economic deprivation and political grievances that fuel piracy and smuggling. This balance reflects the ongoing challenge of securing the Strait of Hormuz while respecting the complex political and economic realities of the Gulf region. Effective maritime security around the Strait of Hormuz depends not only on robust patrols, but also on tackling the underlying causes of instability. Enhanced economic cooperation, anti-corruption measures against smuggling, and investments in coastal community development can reduce incentives for illicit activities, highlighting the need for a flexible and adaptive approach. Responses should align with evolving threats and regional dynamics as the geopolitical landscape shifts. Awareness of the diverse actors in the waters and their motivations helps tailor effective and sustainable interventions, fostering a more secure maritime environment.

4
Strategic Military Capabilities and Deployments

Naval Power and Maritime Defence Systems of Gulf Countries

The states of the Arabian Gulf, with their strategic foresight, maintain a constellation of naval forces that is increasingly sophisticated and multifunctional. This serves as a cornerstone of both internal and transnational maritime security. The Kingdom of Saudi Arabia, the United Arab Emirates, the State of Qatar, and the Sultanate of Oman, among others, have pursued systematic capital-intensive programmes to modernise and expand surface, subsurface, and auxiliary fleets. This proactive approach addresses a range of security challenges, including asymmetric threats and conventional state rivalries. The countries' geographic alignment along the Arabian Gulf, and specifically the border coinciding with the Strait of Hormuz—a critical maritime artery accounting for a significant fraction of global hydrocarbon shipments—renders the permanent projection and protection of naval power an indispensable national and collective strategic objective.

Consequently, the procurement and operational sustainment of advanced maritime defence systems are accorded unequivocal priority within defence planning frameworks. Gulf naval modernisation measures are configured to create a layered defence architecture integrating corvette and frigate squadrons, mobile coastal and missile platforms, persistent air and underwater surveillance vectors, and a comprehensive command-control-information implications coalition. The operational emphasis on indigenous production capacities, advanced foreign technology, and knowledge transfer is matched by declining surface-ship acquisition, command and signalling systems. Regionally, strategic dialogue, practical interoperability training, and joint exercises with established maritime powers have entrenched multinational security co-operation as a principal variable in Gulf maritime security architecture. This regional cooperation is a beacon of hope for stability in the region. The cumulative implications of these developments constitute a distinctive balance of maritime forces, systematically evolving towards the collective prevention of sea denial, the sustainment of choke-point security, and the enhancement of the collective ability to respond to emergent threats.

The continued modernisation of naval forces not only underpins the enhancement of the Gulf states' security architecture but also recalibrates their strategic calculus within the wider Indo-Pacific theatre. Participating in recurring COMBINED Task Force exercises, alongside the United States and NATO partners, sharpens crew proficiency, doctrinal commonality, and technological interoperability—threads critical to conducting persistent surveillance and power projection in the Strait. Concurrent expenditures to construct forward operating bases, expand and digitise port facilities, and integrate command-and-control nodes linked to the Gulf Maritime Security Operations Centre signal an irreversible commitment to raising naval operational ceilings and sustaining a credible forward deterrent. This commitment is a testament to the region's defence capabilities and readiness.

Contestation for naval patrimony and strategic discourse in the Gulf has crystallised the perception that a credible maritime doctrine is a prerequisite for unimpeded access and for signalling deterrent capability to external and maritime proxy forces. The extent to which Washington supports a sanctions-dependent, foreign-user naval architecture complicates the calculus, as Persian Gulf states seek to consolidate asymmetric deterrents without an irretrievable over-reliance on foreign carriers, weapons systems, and operational frameworks. Therefore, maritime security dialogue must be weighed against coerced observations and foreign troops that encumber a rationale of strategic gradation.

The concurrent pursuit of regular, reciprocal engagement, information networks to feed sensor-to-shooter triangles, permanent liaison, and linked watch-keeping among regional navies stands as a tacit answer to anticipatory rivalry. Consequently, a persistent Gulf naval construct will be tested in real-time by the degree to which naval commanders prioritise the synchronisation of day-to-day readiness training alongside commercially created, open bilateral engagements—observable only when deliberate shows of force do not mutate into open deterrent miscalibration. Therefore, the operational continuity now underway in the Strait will be cemented only to the extent that state navies expand their operational modus operandi constructively.

Fostering trust and transparency among regional stakeholders is instrumental for reinforcing collective security. It affirms the necessity of a coordinated response to the naval challenges that confront the area, and underscores the importance of cooperation in maintaining regional stability.

The Role of External Military Presence and Alliances

The Strait of Hormuz constitutes a vital artery for global energy security, serving as the sole maritime channel connecting the Persian Gulf to the open ocean. Approximately one-fifth of the world's crude oil passes through the Strait daily, making it a crucial choke point for international trade and lubricant supplies. Its geopolitical and economic significance has prompted various external powers to sustain a military presence in the waterway to guarantee the unimpeded flow of commerce and the safeguarding of national interests.

To that end, the external military posture typically encompasses naval task forces, fixed and mobile air bases, and layered maritime surveillance assets, thus providing the capacity for timely escalation and crisis response. These deployments are calibrated not only to dissuade potential aggressors but also to furnish the littoral states with a tangible security guarantee, thereby reinforcing the regional equilibrium in the face of persistent friction. Among the principal external contributors are the United States, the United Kingdom, and France, as well as regional powers with overseas military assets, such as India and China, in more limited capacities.

The Fifth Fleet, headquartered in Bahrain, constitutes a standing maritime force devoted to protracted surveillance of the Strait of Hormuz and its adjoining maritime zones. This continual deployment facilitates expedited crisis management, historically exemplified by the swift operational reactions to the 2019 assaults on commercial tankers. Complementary to American holdings, the British Royal Navy routinely allocates naval task groups—effectively carrier strike and surface escort units—operating episodically from logistic hubs in the United Arab Emirates. Such rotations inject enhanced deterrent and reassurance effects.

French maritime engagement, through the dispatch of surface escorts, amphibious units, and maritime patrol aviation, further exemplifies multilateral resoluteness. The Force d'Intervention Rapide and carrier groups have participated in coalition formations to police strategic choke points, driven by the imperative to protect supply lines to the collectively administered overseas departments and critical hydrocarbon interests. Interoperable drills, maritime situational awareness fusion, and stealthy strategic signal sharing collectively institutionalise confidence. Notwithstanding the operational benefits, the persistent stationing of non-regional naval assets injects tensions into discourses of sovereign prerogatives and emergent aspirations for regional autonomy, the cumulative weight of which imposes a continuous diplomatic management burden.

While the cooperation agreements offered by global military powers—in particular the United States—are broadly received as vital security supplements by the Gulf monarchies, an imperative invariably tempers acceptance to safeguard domestic authority and circumscribed agency. The deployment of large external military contingents is frequently interpreted as encroachment upon the sovereign space of the domestic military, legal, and political spheres. Incidents of lethargy, misalignment, or overt military manipulation by the foreign contingent, especially when the strategic intention is calibrated to advance an external narrative, tend to reinforce the conviction that state autonomy is being compromised. A prominent manifestation of this friction is the episodic escalation of proxy hostilities, whereby mission-dominant external forces literally and figuratively recontract the regional alignment of forces, thereby altering the standing regional equilibrium as perceived by local security elites.

Within the Gulf basin, the equilibrium is frequently refracted through the prisms of external alignment. Principal states—like Saudi Arabia, the United Arab Emirates, and, to an extent, Qatar and Oman—effectively stratify tiered pools of access and influence over growing orchestral tasks contingent upon the degree of doctrinal intimacy with NATO and GCC states. Those monarchies which are confidently anchored to American and European forces can monetise policy preferences into a discreet military doctrine, cushioning themselves against regional dependencies. Conversely, states shielded from close doctrinal union are, from time to time, left to mediate between competing wider policies. Consequently, exposure to divergent transnational normative paradigms revamps the terms of conditional equilibrium, reshaping linear decision-making over military, economic, or diplomatic resources. The melt of divergent external modalities of posture and grievance during the barbed hostilities that have scarred the Gulf, indubitably recasts the architecture.

External military interventions can inadvertently intensify existing conflicts by layering new rivalries onto already complex local dynamics. The states of the Gulf Cooperation Council (GCC) consistently recalibrate their foreign military engagements, alternating between collaboration and rivalry, to secure core national interests while simultaneously managing relationships with non-regional powers according to self-determined objectives. An ongoing tactical consideration is the deliberate effort by GCC governments to supplement foreign military footprints with the systematic expansion of indigenous military capacities.

Growing national budgets that support domestic armed forces and the incremental establishment of indigenous defence production capacities represent deliberate incremental steps towards diminished strategic dependence, although the states concerned continue to derive tangible security benefits from existing strategic alliances. This dual-track security model is thus indispensable for maintaining Gulf sovereignty and security amid heightened global media scrutiny and external domestic pressures.

Breakthrough Technologies in Maritime Surveillance and Defence

Gulf states are increasingly applying novel maritime surveillance and defensive systems, innovations that are acquiring decisive strategic weight. Programmes incorporating multimodal asymmetric systems are now proliferating across national budgets, with objectives that extend the monitoring envelope and safeguard convective zones connecting the Arabian Gulf and the broader maritime domain.

Efforts now emphasise high-resolution electro-optical and synthetic aperture satellite constellations, persistent uncrewed aerial vehicles (UAVs) operating across the transnational medium, and complementary autonomous undersea vehicles, each component designed to generate a layered, interoperational sensor architecture. The combination of multi-intelligence collection, multi-domain sensor fusion and backwards-compatible decision-support algorithms promises a calibrated increase in situational awareness, contributing to the deterrence and defence of the Strait of Hormuz, the world's busiest maritime grey-light operating zones.

Affordable and high-precision satellite systems now enable states to track maritime traffic in meticulous real-time across a transcontinental viewing distance. Complementary advances in satellite data-processing algorithms facilitate the automatic classification of vessel types, detection of anomalous operational patterns, and continuous, wide-area surveillance of the Gulf's littoral and open waters. Concurrently, uncrewed aerial vehicles equipped with multi-spectral sensors hover over choke points, delivering live overhead intelligence and collecting tactical data at an operational tempo that outpaces that of conventional maritime patrol vessels.

Autonomous underwater systems undertake near-shore taskings, including submarine track management and minefield reconnaissance, thereby augmenting the scope of regional maritime security efforts. This suite of maritime robotics compresses the sensor-to-shooter timeline, enhancing early warning and shortening reaction cycles, thereby reinforcing the deterrent calculus of states in the area. The bulk of the portfolio is underpinned equally by operational imperatives and by diversification of indigenous defence and security manufacturing.

Gulf states, therefore, have systematically pursued multimodal sensor fusion to safeguard linchpin shipping corridors and minimise exposure to chronic criminal, hybrid, or conventional maritime threats. Multi-frequency, phased-array radar assets, anchored in dense land-borne and offshore platforms, are interoperatively fused with regional communications networks to provide an all-weather, theatre-wide maritime picture. Complementing this, several states are systematically investing in probabilistic artificial intelligence, which ingests the multi-sensor data tapestry and, through deep learning and reasoning, generates threat trajectories, ranks probable denial-of-access scenarios, and furnishes pre-emptive feasibility recommendations.

Predictive analytics distinctly surfaces patterns that portend threats before they actually occur, thereby providing a forward-looking paradigm for securing maritime domains. The prompt assimilation of such technologies is recalibrating national formulations of maritime sovereignty and territorial defence, shifting emphasis toward autonomous, near-real-time computation in operational decision-making that supplements, rather than supersedes, conventional maritime patrols and forward naval presence. While these capabilities undeniably extend the aperture and acuity of maritime surveillance, they concurrently introduce multifaceted strategic dilemmas.

Principal among these dilemmas is the risk that governance over surveillance systems may be disrupted by misinformation or cyber operations, thereby jeopardising the veracity and reliability of operational assessment. Adversarial elements may target the satellite uplink, manipulate sensor fusion, or turn off autonomous undersea vehicle command and control, thereby generating deceptive operational scenarios or creating persistent sensor denial. Such prospects invite a reconsideration of operational dependency, mandating the embedment of resilient, multilayered cyber defences contemporaneous with the deployment of sophisticated surveillance architecture.

Moreover, the forward deployment of technologically advanced systems within geographies marked by pre-existing diplomatic friction risks exacerbating the security dilemmas of the spiral variety. Neighbouring states are likely to accelerate counter-surveillance platforms or reinforce maritime countermeasure capabilities in anticipatory response, thereby paradoxically enlarging the sensor threat. Regions such as the Persian Gulf, already a locus for sovereignty contests, may witness diplomatic signalling that leverages enhanced surveillance presence, thereby intensifying deterred postures. The coalescence of these inputs raises the risk of inadvertent escalation, as misinterpretations arising from data misclassifications—whether algorithmically or through composite sensor processing—can precipitate unwarranted pre-emptive or reactive military engagement in factual terms.

A further complexity arises in the need to harmonise enhanced regional collaboration with the preservation of sovereign prerogatives. Gulf states are obliged to govern the joint use of sensor and analytic data with exquisite care to avert the hazards of incidental harm and strategic miscalculation. Trust cultivation among state and non-state interlocutors is a strategic necessity; yet, the region's institutional culture of guarded rivalry renders this trust-building process arduous. Diverging interpretative frameworks are emerging: certain authorities regard fused intelligence as a vehicle for a minimalist collective-security architecture. In contrast, others interpret the same data-sharing gesture as a tacit encroachment on sovereign autonomy.

Compounding the matter, the introduction of semi-autonomous and fully autonomous sensor-killer platform combinations generates a lattice of legal and ethical dilemmas centred upon the deployment of artificially invested agents in action-ready scenarios. Autonomous reasoning in kinetic and deterrent patrol operations, for example, raises disputes over the perpetuation of meaningful human control, habitual norms of proportionality, and the persistence of accountability for unlawful harm. Seen from a different analytical angle, the same engineered, pre-synthesisable sensor actuators that increase the circuit's integral deterrent capacity also introduce a set of new attack surfaces and inadvertent triggering mechanisms, including hypothetical misalignments, exhaustive testing, and governance-deep misunderstandings.

5
Threats to Maritime Security in the Strait of Hormuz

Iranian Naval Activities and Asymmetric Warfare Tactics

Iranian naval activity is a cornerstone of its broader strategic calculus, with a particular focus on the Strait of Hormuz, a vital passage through which a substantial share of the world's hydrocarbon shipments transit. To offset the substantial naval predominance enjoyed by the United States and its allied maritime forces, the Islamic Republic has opted decisively for an asymmetric warfare posture. Tehran fields a fleet composed of numerous small, highly mobile surface craft, diesel-electric submarines, and anti-ship missile batteries, enabling it to project influence and impose costs that exceed the limits of its conventional hardware.

A constellation informs the strategic adoption of such asymmetric instruments of enduring geopolitical anxieties. Iranians view the post-2003 transformation in Iraq, coupled with sustained hostilities emanating from neighbouring states, as having elevated the perceived immediacy of American and allied threats. As a force multiplier, asymmetric warfare capitalises upon Tehran's intimate familiarity with the intricacies of the region's littoral geography. It allows for the employment of hit-and-run, enclave-seizing operations modelled upon guerrilla precedents.

This concept of operations has the capacity to induce considerable friction and uncertainty in regional maritime security, thus constraining the effective freedom of action of more powerful surface forces. Mastery of the Strait affords Tehran significant leverage over hydrocarbons destined for foreign markets, thereby consolidating its self-perception as a pivotal regional actor. The Islamic Republic, therefore, structures its strategic narrative around publicly demonstrated exercises that illustrate the reach and precision of its anti-ship capabilities, frequently integrating swarms of speedboats, shore-to-ship anti-ship missiles, and related systems in closely coordinated demonstrations.

These manoeuvres simultaneously underscore Tehran's material capacity and reinforce its claim to regional primacy amid persistent external scrutiny. A current examination of the Islamic Republic's irregular maritime doctrine reveals an adherence to the fundamentals of asymmetric warfare. Iran forwards concentrated detachments of fast-attack craft to interdict, or threaten to interdict, larger opponent units. By compounding speed and quantity, the minor surface force endeavours to paralyse the decision cycles of adversaries expected to employ more conservative reaction protocols.

The introduction of ambiguity in the correlation of forces and diluted maritime conventions permits mission escalation while allowing Iran to characterise operations as defensive. Additional asymmetric techniques materialise in the projection of persistent ambiguity along crucial international shipping arteries. When mined or subjected to drone reconnaissance and limited drone strike operations, these corridors enable uneven escalation, thereby corroding confidence in maritime entitlement while refraining from formally declared hostilities.

Funding limited operations of relatively low cost, Tehran compels adversaries to recalibrate deterrent doctrine and to measure the risk of uncontrolled escalation against the prospect of operational inconvenience. This inverted calculus, in additive tension with the concomitant presentation of deterrence rhetoric, allows Iranian forces to maintain heightened alertness while refraining from costly significant engagement.

Investors, and their respective policy-oriented networks, situated within the strategic ecology of the Gulf, confront these employed tactics as a salient case. Only by accounting for the structured, incremental, and often deniable character of Iranian threat formulation may broader maritime assurance choreography incorporate a corrupt regional equilibrium, accommodating the persistent dialectic of deterrent strength and deterrent economy executed by the Islamic Republic.

Piracy, Smuggling, and Non-State Actor Interventions

The Strait of Hormuz remains an essential maritime bottleneck, whose enduring security dilemmas reverberate through both regional economies and the global trading system. Criminal behaviour—specifically piracy and smuggling—continues systematically to impair the safe transit of vessels through the waterway, influencing not only states bordering the Gulf but also the wider international community. These threats originate from a heterogeneous array of actors, ranging from opportunistic bandits who pursue high-value tonnage to organised smuggling syndicates transporting munitions, hydrocarbons, and other contraband across the exact domains.

Non-state armed formations, intentionally or opportunistically, superimpose an additional strategic dimension. Such groups frequently meander through the channel for purposes that advance either a clearly defined ideological project or the narrower pursuit of illicit economic gain. Their intermittent interference has aggravated the already intricate balance of power among Gulf states, producing an elevated state of alert for merchant vessels whose voyage plans must reckon with a corporatised reliance on the corridor for transits of displaced Iranian and Gulf hydrocarbon exports. Regional contraband contravenes national law and emerges as an abbreviated lens through which to scrutinise extant geopolitical dissension and foreign economic sanction regimes.

The continuous exploitation of clandestine transit by compact, agile craft facilitates the covert transport of contraband, including narcotics, alongside an expanding inventory of prohibited materials. Such clandestine convoys systematically erode compliant economic sectors while providing sustained fiscal backing to enterprises that progressively endanger regional stability. Concurrently, incidents of piratical aggression, although markedly lower than elsewhere—especially in the Gulf of Aden—nonetheless pose a persistent and damaging risk to commercial maritime traffic. Evidence of vulnerable regional maritime layers now indicates that segments of the piratical array have begun to receive overt or tacit support from broader, non-state political actors. This worrisome convergence sufficiently liquidates the inherence of a discrete criminal culture, ceding leverage to political militancy and proliferating more sophisticated, operationally lethal regulatory gaps. Periods of naval engagement fragmentation, a direct by-product of operational strain and concurrent, multiplicative, corridor obligations, furnish openings that these actors recurrently exploit, subsequently exposing prolific deficiencies in bilateral and multilateral maritime governance. The resultant maritime insecurity, moreover, exerts economically infectious, multiphase ramifications that extend to the level of national economies. Disruptions to vessel throughput in the Strait of Hormuz correlate demonstrably to abrupt, telegraphed movements in global hydrocarbon pricing, imparting an uneven, incidental pressure on the intricately interlinked energy and transport sectors. Member countries of the Gulf Cooperation Council, whose fiscal and monetary foundations remain critically tied to saturated maritime transit, therefore confront tangible risks to macroeconomic equilibrium and the perception of stable credit systems. Similarly, liability underwriters, multinational elevating fleets, and hinterland connections now routinely quantify the marked escalation in risk-pricing determinants, as evidenced by elevated coverage, departure offsets, and marginal increases in the absorption of freight premiums and expediting delays, collectively enacting a covert elevation of economic marginalism and system costs.

Non-state actors in the Gulf environment neither operate in a domestic vacuum nor restrict their activities within recognised national borders, so their presence has the dual effect of aggravating the security landscape and encroaching upon the sovereignty of littoral states. Their operations frequently serve as instruments of broader geopolitical rivalries, with external patrons supplying arms, training, or other forms of support to achieve indirect leverage. Such dynamics necessitate a level of granularity in analysis that must inform both the strategic circles within the Gulf and the broader scholarship devoted to the region's security, as well as the norms governing the high seas. Gulf littoral states have, in consequence, deployed a graduated response to the security erosion affecting the Strait of Hormuz, including the deployment of naval assets, refinement of domestic and international regulatory frameworks, and integration of advanced surveillance systems. The United Arab Emirates, the Kingdom of Saudi Arabia, and the Sultanate of Oman have in particular augmented their coastal missile batteries, corvette squadrons, and offshore patrol craft to restore a credible defensive perimeter. Concurrently, regular multilateral naval exercises and intelligence fusion operations serve to harmonise tactics, procedures, and information among the national fleets. Those initiatives are, in practical terms, buttressed by allied navies, notably those of the United States and the United Kingdom, as well as successive multinational coalitions that station carrier strike groups, maritime patrol aircraft, and combination fleets to deter predatory behaviours while reassuring the maritime trade that transits the world's foremost choke point. The challenge lies in calibrating the presence to achieve an acceptable level of deterrence without risking an openly hostile stance. Complementary diplomatic packaging has been of equal significance in maintaining a delicate balance between the identified need for enhanced security and the legitimate aspirations of the littoral states to manage their territorial seas without external supervision.

The member states of the Gulf Cooperation Council pragmatically engage with established global regimes, such as the International Maritime Organisation, and consistently implement applicable United Nations conventions to affirm their maritime entitlements and encourage cooperative security arrangements. Several states within the Council have subsequently pursued the formation of focused maritime task forces and platforms for the real-time exchange of intelligence, geared to counter piracy and illicit trafficking while intentionally restraining the use of military force. These initiatives are calibrated to the strategic awareness that the Strait of Hormuz, as a vital juncture, entails a delicate balance—excessive or overtly foreign military presence may compromise national sovereignty. In contrast, insufficient preventive coordination of national and external efforts may create significant security gaps.

Simultaneously, relevant foreign governance and institutional stakeholders deliberate on providing strategic, measured assistance. Such support encompasses scalable development of maritime assistance capabilities, the transfer of surveillance technologies, and synchronised exchanges with commercial shipping networks to elevate threat perception and management. Regional diplomats and security cognoscenti underscore that unhindered, although discreet, dialogue between divergent Gulf actors—both public and private—remains vital to minimising interpretive missteps and averting unintended military escalation.

Several Gulf states pursue restrained channels of dialogue with select neighbouring non-state actors, aiming, where practical, to tackle drivers such as chronic economic marginalisation and unresolved political grievances that underpin robbery-at-sea and contraband activity. This diplomatic calculus exemplifies the persistent effort to manage Strait of Hormuz security while honouring the unresolved institutional and socioeconomic asymmetries of the region, and it underscores the premise that durable deterrence rests not solely on naval formations but on tactical initiatives that stabilise the maritime hinterland. Strategic resilience around the Strait therefore seeks, synchronously and proportionally, to fortify surface and aerial sealing operations while engaging upstream sources of insecurity. Programmatic expansion of selective economic interdependence, the application of governance reforms that starve corruption-linked smuggling nodes, and a tightly calibrated portfolio of diaspora-engaged port and ancillary village investment collectively diminish the opportunistic calculus that covert transgressors may otherwise default to. Accordingly, a posture of strategic adaptability—incremental calibration against the cyclical and emergent profile of threats—has become a requisite governance lever. Continuing to map the developing mosaic of actors and their incentive architectures, then, allows a calibrated, graduated, and proportionate response that consequently deters yet prudently contains escalation. Securing consistent and unobstructed carriage within this artery ultimately sustains the dependable throughput on which both regional and extra-regional constituencies rely for livelihood security and for stability of the larger, interwoven supply chains.

Potential Conventional and Non-Conventional Threat Scenarios

Generally speaking, conventional threats to regional stability mainly involve military or semi-military actions. A primary concern is maritime interdiction, where a country (or a non-state actor) tries to restrict the movement of ships, especially through the Strait of Hormuz, a vital choke point for oil (Pugliese G, 2022). During conflicts, such actions can be a strategic play, intended to disrupt oil supplies or put economic pressure on nations. Piracy also poses a risk in the Gulf waters, particularly during periods of instability or reduced naval patrolling, which threatens shipping lanes and energy markets. Additionally, potential military confrontations—whether among regional powers or involving external actors—pose significant threats. These conflicts might stem from territorial disputes or the quest for strategic dominance, and could escalate into open hostilities, disrupting maritime traffic and endangering economic stability (Kupriyanov A.V., 2022).

Graphic (1)

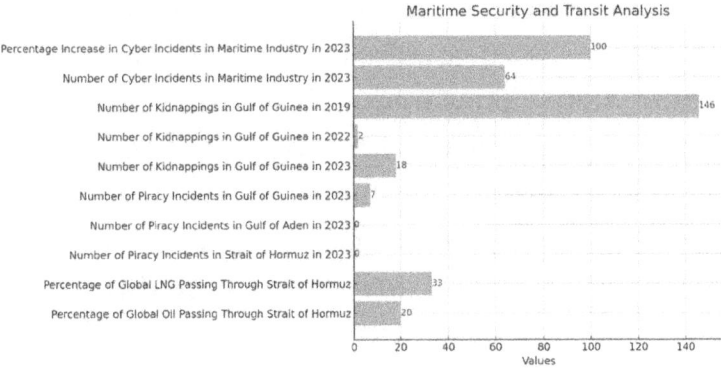

This chart illustrates various aspects of maritime security and transit. It highlights the significant percentages of global oil and LNG traffic through the Strait of Hormuz, while indicating a notably low number of piracy incidents in that region for 2023. In contrast, the Gulf of Guinea experienced multiple piracy incidents and a concerning rise in kidnappings, demonstrating the evolving threats in maritime security. Additionally, there was a significant increase in cyber incidents within the maritime industry, marking a critical area of concern for security strategies. (Cyber attacks on shipping rise amid geopolitical tensions, Financial Times 2025).

If these risks materialise, they could lead to major disruptions in global energy supplies, necessitating preparedness and early deterrence. Non-conventional threats differ, targeting security through methods not directly tied to traditional warfare. Asymmetric warfare is a growing challenge; here, smaller actors use covert tactics to offset disadvantages against more powerful opponents. For instance, irregular groups might use hit-and-run raids or sabotage in the Gulf, destabilising the area or causing chaos, thus undermining local governance. The danger from terrorist activities is persistent, with potential targeting of oil infrastructure, naval vessels, or ports to cause panic and economic damage.

Furthermore, cyber-attacks have emerged as a new front. Hackers or state-sponsored entities can disrupt maritime communication, interfere with navigation, or disable control centres of oil platforms and shipping operations. Such methods are often hard to trace and can be executed remotely, making them particularly insidious. These threats can undermine regional stability without resorting to military confrontation, compelling states to develop comprehensive defence strategies that address both physical and cyber vulnerabilities. Another form of non-conventional threat involves propaganda and information warfare. State or non-state actors might spread false information to influence public opinion, destabilise governments, or manipulate market perceptions of energy resources. Economic sanctions and trade restrictions are also employed as non-military tools to exert pressure without resorting to direct violence. However, they can still inflict significant damage on regional economies. The rise of unmanned aerial vehicles (UAVs), also known as drones, adds another threat, capable of reconnaissance or attacks on key facilities such as oil terminals or warships. These non-conventional approaches often work in tandem with traditional threats, creating scenarios that necessitate adaptive, multi-layered security responses. Recognising these diverse threats and their potential impacts is essential for policymakers, especially as tech continues to evolve rapidly.

6
Regional Autonomy and Sovereignty Concerns

Balancing National Sovereignty with Collective Security Arrangements

Generally speaking, when discussing maritime security and regional autonomy, particularly in key areas such as the Strait of Hormuz, it is crucial to consider the delicate balance between a nation's right to govern itself and the need for countries to collaborate for security. The Strait acts as a vital point for global trade and energy, which understandably brings in a significant amount of foreign military activity. This can sometimes step on the toes of the countries that border the Strait, as they often have overlapping claims to the area (Faculty of the Department of Affairs NS et al., 1998). This foreign influence adds complexity to the region. Local governments find themselves in a challenging position, attempting to maintain their authority while also safeguarding their maritime borders against potential threats, whether from other countries or non-state actors. Moreover, as we have seen with Sri Lanka's maritime situation, the competing desires of bigger nations—given how important its waters are for global shipping—combined with the inherent vulnerabilities of smaller countries, really highlight the tension between pursuing regional autonomy and accepting security help from outside (Kumara et al., 2021). This mix of interests not only underscores the need for a profound, nuanced grasp of what sovereignty truly means, but also urges us to find creative policy answers. These solutions should both respect local governance and address the shared challenges to maritime security.

Gulf nations are increasingly recognising the necessity of safeguarding their sovereignty, even as they participate in collective security endeavours (Faculty of the Department of Affairs, NS et al., 1998). The Strait of Hormuz, a vital waterway, facilitates a substantial portion—roughly 20%—of the world's oil trade (□□□, 2023). Geopolitical tensions prevalent in the region, particularly those arising from state and non-state actors, compel Gulf countries to prioritise their national interests. Consequently, they engage selectively with international security frameworks, such as the Gulf Cooperation Council (GCC), or broader alliances with powers like the United States. Each nation delicately juggles enhancing its sovereignty with participating in collective defence strategies designed to address shared security concerns. The stakes are considerable for Gulf states. The safe passage of oil tankers and regional stability often depend on collaboration with other states; however, such collaboration must respect national autonomy. A growing number of Gulf countries are investing in their military capabilities to augment diplomatic efforts, thereby asserting their sovereignty and reducing their reliance on external powers. Strategic alliances providing collective security assurances while respecting national sovereignty are, therefore, critical in this geopolitical environment. As Gulf nations seek a balance between national autonomy and collective security, specific challenges arise. A particularly pressing concern involves tensions between national and collective interests. In engaging with security agreements, Gulf countries must consider whether these agreements may limit their ability to act independently during crises. This balance proves especially relevant in disputes over maritime trade routes, where national interests sometimes diverge considerably. Regional security arrangements can sometimes feel more like a source of pressure than a genuine cooperative effort. For instance, some Gulf nations might feel compelled to support collective military actions that may not fully align with their strategic objectives.

Furthermore, internal politics and public opinion can complicate the decision-making process. Leaders must navigate domestic expectations that demand a strong national stance, all the while assessing the benefits of collective action for security and stability. To navigate these complexities, Gulf nations need to undertake careful strategic planning. This might involve prioritising security collaborations aimed explicitly at mitigating external threats, concurrently investing in national defence capabilities. By cultivating a sense of security from within, these countries may better navigate the pressures of collective agreements while protecting their sovereignty. Collaborative military exercises, shared intelligence systems, and diplomatic dialogues offer viable ways for Gulf countries to combine their efforts without compromising their independence.

In most cases, the relationship between national sovereignty and collective security in the Gulf is a dynamic and evolving one. Nations recognise that partnerships can offer mutual benefits while respecting individual aspirations for autonomy. As these dynamics unfold, sustained dialogue among Gulf states will be crucial for developing a harmonious approach to collective security arrangements that promotes both regional stability and national integrity.

Impact of External Interventions on Regional Autonomy

Gulf nations often find their ability to fully control their territorial waters limited, particularly in strategic maritime chokepoints like the Strait of Hormuz, due to external interventions. This narrow passage, vital for global oil shipments, attracts numerous global powers eager to secure their economic and security interests (Selth, A., 2022). Indeed, many external actors frequently deploy military bases and naval forces within or near Gulf waters, using surveillance technologies. Justified, usually, under the banner of security or freedom of navigation, such measures, in most cases, impose constraints on the sovereignty of Gulf states over their own maritime domains. The presence disrupts traditional governance structures and challenges the authority of local regimes to independently manage, regulate, and protect these critical areas. Foreign powers' influence in the Gulf has also introduced policies and strategic frameworks—shaped more by outside interests than by the regional states themselves (D J B Smith et al., 2022). Decisions concerning maritime security and oil transit protocols often reflect the priorities of external actors, like the United States, Britain, or China, rather than the actual needs or ambitions of the Gulf countries. Generally speaking, external control can restrict the capacity of Gulf states to form policies tailored to their unique socio-political contexts. Moreover, it can foster a sense of external Dependency; Gulf nations may feel pressured to align their policies with the expectations of these powerful foreign presences rather than pursuing fully independent courses of action. The geopolitical environment in which Gulf states operate is continually shaped by external involvement.

For instance, the presence of foreign naval fleets and military alliances impacts how these countries negotiate territorial rights or manage disputes within the Gulf. Tensions within the region arise as countries attempt to balance foreign influence with their own national interests. Efforts by Gulf countries to maintain regional stability and assert their authority over critical maritime corridors are complicated by the geopolitical complexities introduced by external actors. The broad influence of external powers presents substantial challenges to the regional autonomy of Gulf nations. Dependency on foreign military protection and diplomatic backing often comes at the price of reduced self-determination, a situation that undermines traditional regional authority, particularly where local rulers historically exercised direct control over security and governance. Entrenched with strategic assets, external actors cause Gulf states to adjust their policies and alliances, sometimes compromising aspects of their sovereignty to maintain security assurances.

This scenario has pushed Gulf countries to seek more autonomous security frameworks that rely less on external powers. While alliances remain important, a growing movement among Gulf governments aims to develop their own military capabilities and diplomatic networks, consider investments in national defence industries, expanded regional cooperation, and cultivating broader partnerships beyond traditional Western allies. Such moves reflect an ambition to balance the leverage of external alliances with a stronger sense of self-reliance, aiming to safeguard national and regional interests while avoiding excessive dependence. At the same time, Gulf countries continue to navigate a delicate balance between maintaining these external relationships and expanding their independent voices.

The Gulf region often grapples with the perceived limitations that external alliances place on its policy independence, a point underscored by studies examining Gulf state relationships (Shaheen et al., 2025). That being said, it is almost impossible for these states to isolate themselves completely, given the current nature of global politics. This necessity for balance significantly influences the political and economic choices made in the Gulf currently, as governments strive to maximise the benefits of external alliances while preserving their own sovereignty and leadership roles (Shaheen et al., 2025). For instance, responses to regional security threats and global changes often mirror this dynamic. We often see Gulf countries embracing increased foreign intervention during tense times, viewing it as protection from external threats, and this has played out in recent situations.

On the other hand, when regional powers attempt to expand their influence, Gulf states seek to exert more control over their own strategic assets and military, illustrating the ongoing push and pull between external forces and national interests. This constant negotiation—mainly driven by external actors, especially considering the growing influence of Asian powers —aims to assert regional autonomy. To truly understand the Gulf's role in global affairs, policymakers and academics must carefully observe how these external interventions intersect with regional autonomy; this interplay remains a defining feature of Gulf politics. Gulf leaders need to consider how foreign presence affects not only their security but also their ability to act independently, as it has significant implications for their geopolitical strategies. This understanding is crucial for developing sustainable strategies that take into account both regional dynamics and the realities of global politics, ensuring that Gulf countries manage their external relationships in a manner that preserves their sovereignty and regional significance.

Case Studies of Autonomy Challenges in Gulf States

The Gulf states navigate a complex situation, balancing their own sovereignty with the need to manage external security threats, particularly in the Strait of Hormuz, a strategically vital waterway. Because the region relies on this Strait for its oil exports and international trade, it is a centre of global interest, often drawing external powers into the mix (Faculty of the Department of Affairs NS et al., 1998). Historically, significant actors such as the United States and Iran have wielded influence in the Gulf, occasionally posing challenges to the individual autonomy of the Gulf states. Iran's continuous endeavours to assert its influence in the Strait and adjacent regions, for instance, have placed neighbouring countries under pressure to align with external security agendas (Ostrom et al., 2021). These external pressures limit the capacity of Gulf states to independently formulate and execute their own security strategies, without the risk of conflicts or diplomatic repercussions. Instances such as Iran's threatening maritime manoeuvres or the U.S. military presence illustrate how external security concerns frequently take precedence over regional autonomy, compelling Gulf states into intricate diplomatic and strategic compromises.

Furthermore, regional conflicts and rivalries exacerbate

challenges to sovereignty. The 2017 Gulf Cooperation Council (GCC) crisis, during which several countries blockaded Qatar, is a prime example of how such disputes can undermine collective regional autonomy. This crisis underscored the intertwined nature of external and internal factors, as external powers tend to favour specific states, thereby influencing their policies and security alliances. External actors might, in some cases, exploit regional disputes to rationalise military interventions or heighten security measures, further restricting the independence of Gulf states. Consequently, Gulf countries often find they have to recalibrate their foreign policies to navigate the influence of external actors, all while striving to protect their sovereignty. There is an ongoing tension, generally speaking, between regional security imperatives and the desire to maintain autonomy.

Sovereignty Challenges in the Gulf

In the Gulf, autonomous decision-making remains a crucial element shaping regional geopolitics. These issues reveal that sovereignty is not simply a matter of a nation's internal affairs; instead, it is usually a complex interplay of external influences and, of course, security concerns. Often, the strategic interests of external powers in the region lead to compromises regarding the independence of Gulf states, which makes it difficult for them to control their foreign policy and security decisions fully (Karim A et al., 2023). Recognising these external pressures is essential for understanding the tensions currently unfolding in the Strait of Hormuz and the broader Gulf region, where external security imperatives frequently test sovereignty. Kuwait, for instance, has managed a delicate position within the Gulf by balancing its security needs alongside its sovereignty. The 1991 Gulf War served as a stark reminder of external threats and the critical importance of external security guarantees, which many Kuwaitis see as essential for their continued independence.

Despite this reliance, Kuwait has maintained a firm internal policy aimed at preserving its sovereignty by developing a relatively open and independent foreign policy, wherever and whenever possible. In regional conflicts, a cautious approach is often taken, avoiding alignment with extreme positions to safeguard its internal stability and autonomy. Bahrain's situation highlights exactly how internal security and external influences can directly impact sovereignty. This small island nation has experienced drawn-out unrest driven by a majority population belonging to the Shiite community, yet ruled by a Sunni monarchy. External influences, especially from neighbouring Iran, play a role in this unrest; Tehran is often accused of meddling in Bahrain's internal affairs.

Meanwhile, Bahrain's security strategy heavily depends on the support of regional and Western allies, primarily through the deployment of U.S. naval forces and security agreements with neighbouring Gulf Cooperation Council countries. This external reliance complicates Bahrain's autonomy, as its political stability and, indeed, sovereignty, are intertwined with external security arrangements. The need for external guarantees against regional threats and internal unrest frequently overshadows efforts to assert independence. Qatar presents a somewhat different case: a country with a small population that has gained international prominence via its independent foreign policy, regional mediations, and economic strategies. The decision to host the U.S. drone base and maintain diverse international relations has often been viewed as a move to preserve its sovereignty amid increasing regional tensions. Led by Saudi Arabia and the UAE, the blockade by neighbouring Gulf countries in 2017 aimed to pressure Qatar into more closely aligning with their regional policies. Qatar's response involved reinforcing its sovereignty through increased diplomatic engagement, enhanced economic resilience, and diversifying its international partnerships. This approach has enabled Qatar to maintain a degree of independence, despite external efforts to influence its policies. Its experience underscores how small states can attempt to assert sovereignty by balancing external pressures via strategic diplomacy, alongside economic independence. These individual cases demonstrate that Gulf states are, undoubtedly, continuously navigating their sovereignty within a context marked by external influences, regional rivalries, and, most definitely, security imperatives. Kuwait relies on external security guarantees while simultaneously seeking to maintain internal autonomy. Bahrain's sovereignty faces internal unrest as well as external meddling. Qatar's independent foreign policy underscores the inherent complexity of sovereignty issues as they exist in the region.

7
Economic Dimensions of Maritime Security

Oil and Gas Transit Security and Its Economic Implications

The Strait of Hormuz, a strategically vital waterway situated between Oman and Iran, serves as a crucial artery for a substantial portion of the world's oil and gas. Approximately 20% of the planet's oil consumption passes through this narrow passage, underscoring its profound impact on global energy security (Brewster et al., 2014).

Indeed, nations like Saudi Arabia, Iraq, and the United Arab Emirates are profoundly reliant on this strait for exporting their petroleum, making it a vital economic lifeline. Consequently, disruptions here could have far-reaching reverberations. This reliance, though, begets vulnerabilities that demand the attention of nations dependent on the transit of oil and gas; the geopolitics surrounding the Strait of Hormuz only heighten this significance. Political unease among regional actors, particularly regarding Iran, amplifies maritime security concerns; the threat of conflict or terrorism holds the potential to impact shipping directly. Such potential threats could send prices soaring and also disrupt global supply chains, inevitably complicating the already fragile energy situation. For nations dependent on reliable energy supplies, increased security measures, insurance, and logistical planning become essential, adding to the costs of passage through the Strait (Shaheen et al., 2025).

The prospect of instability highlights the profound interconnection between energy security and economic well-being. Moreover, increased maritime security efforts within the Gulf significantly alter the region's trade dynamics. As threats to shipping intensify, nations and companies respond with amplified security protocols. This response typically entails naval deployments, advanced monitoring systems, and greater collaboration between regional allies, all designed to secure these critical shipping lanes. Although vital, these protective measures can increase operational costs, which may ultimately be passed on to consumers. For industries heavily dependent on oil and gas, these added costs can translate to elevated energy product prices, affecting areas ranging from transportation to heating.

Table (5): Economic Impact of Strait of Hormuz on Global Oil and Gas Trade (Administration UEI, 2024)

Year	Oil Flow (million barrels per day)	Percentage of Global Oil Trade	LNG Flow (million tonnes per year)	Percentage of Global LNG Trade
2023	20.9	20%	Approximately 200	20%
2025	Data not specified	27%	Data not specified	22%

Impact of Maritime Disruptions on Global Markets

A key point to remember is the Strait of Hormuz's role in global energy—it's one of the busiest oil routes around. Approximately 20% of the planet's petroleum passes through this small section of sea, connecting major oil producers in the Gulf to the rest of the world, underscoring its strategic importance, particularly in international trade and security (Lortie et al., 2015). Now, when things go wrong—geopolitical issues, military problems, accidents, what have you—oil prices usually jump up fast. The reason is that markets dislike supply threats, which bring uncertainty and higher oil prices; thus, the area is critical for economic stability. Besides just price increases, these interruptions can delay or halt oil and gas shipments. This, in turn, makes energy markets even more unstable and affects economies worldwide.

Table (6): Impact of Maritime Disruptions on Global Markets (USITC, 2025)

Impact Type	Value
Global Maritime Trade Volume Loss	7.0% to 9.6% decrease during the first eight months of 2020
Global Maritime Trade Volume Loss (Tonnes)	Approximately 206 to 286 million tonnes
Global Maritime Trade Value Loss (USD)	Up to 225 to 412 billion USD
Containerized Imports in the U.S. (2020)	7.0% decline in the first half; 9.5% increase in the second half compared to 2019
Shipping Container Leasing Rates Increase	80% rise since early November 2020
Shipping Container Leasing Rates Increase (Year-over-Year)	Nearly tripled over the past year
Port Schedule Reliability	Dropped from 80% to 30% since the beginning of 2020
Port Waiting and Turnaround Times	Increased, particularly in U.S. ports

Shipments significantly impact energy availability, and their ripple effects extend far beyond just oil. The economic consequences, though indirect, are felt across industries that rely on petroleum either as raw materials or energy. Disruptions, therefore, lead to higher costs or shortages, causing a global economic slowdown in both production and trade. Shipping costs are a good example; they rise as insurance premiums go up for ships travelling through dangerous waters, which forces some companies to reroute their cargo along routes that are both longer and more expensive. These changes can cause shortages in essential materials, such as plastics and even fertilisers (Wu H et al., 2020).

The Strait of Hormuz, in particular, has a significant impact on financial markets in regions that heavily rely on oil revenues, specifically the Gulf states. This leads to market volatility that affects investments, currency stability, and economic growth even far outside the immediate maritime region.

Maritime disruptions create challenges for global logistics networks, which rely on the reliable transportation of seaborne cargo. Many products come from Asia and the Gulf or are en route to Europe and the Americas. Delays are inevitable, which in turn affect manufacturing schedules and, ultimately, consumer markets worldwide. Nations along these routes have a lot at stake. Because maritime insccurity is so unpredictable, some countries have begun strategically stockpiling oil reserves and adjusting their suppliers to reduce reliance on Gulf oil (Wang X et al., 2020). These actions reflect the awareness that even short disruptions can have extensive financial and social consequences. It is essential to note that the challenges in the Gulf also involve striking a balance between strategic autonomy and ensuring global economic stability through secure maritime corridors.

Gulf states must address threats and challenges within their waters, protecting their sovereignty while supporting the uninterrupted flow of goods. These goods are crucial not only to their own economies but also to many other countries around the world. Typically, enhanced maritime security includes joint naval patrols, collaborations with international partners, and investments in advanced monitoring technologies. However, these must be managed carefully, as they could prevent escalating tensions or contribute to a militarisation that, strangely enough, could undermine stability. Regional cooperation among Gulf nations, as well as with international stakeholders, is crucial for maintaining open sea lanes. This requires trust, coordination, and aligning interests.

The Gulf countries have increasingly emphasised their role as responsible stewards of these essential shipping lanes, participating actively in dialogues and establishing frameworks to ensure safety. At the same time, some states are adopting independent security policies that reflect unique strategic priorities, potentially complicating collective efforts. Successfully navigating these competing objectives calls for diplomatic skill and a long-term vision. This vision acknowledges both the significance of sovereign control and the economic interdependence that maritime trade fosters. Secure maritime corridors in the Gulf do more than just support regional prosperity; they contribute to global economic stability, reinforcing the link between local security and worldwide markets. Disruptions in these waters have a direct impact on the global energy supply, and miscalculations have the potential to trigger broader economic shocks. Gulf countries must strike a balance between investing in their naval capabilities and pursuing diplomatic engagement to ensure that critical supply routes remain accessible. For global actors, supporting Gulf maritime security while respecting the autonomy of states represents a challenge. Effectively managing this equilibrium is necessary for diminishing the risk of economic disruptions.

Investment in Maritime Infrastructure and Security Technologies

The Strait of Hormuz, which connects the Persian Gulf to the Gulf of Oman and then to the Arabian Sea, is undeniably crucial. Roughly a fifth of the world's traded oil passes through this narrow waterway, underscoring its importance for global energy supplies (Ostrom et al., 2021). Disruptions here, due to political tension or security concerns, can easily reverberate through global markets. To better manage traffic and lessen vulnerabilities, nations might consider investing in maritime infrastructure. This could mean upgraded ports, better navigational aids, and dedicated transit corridors, further emphasising the need for a solid strategic presence (N/A, 2022). Such investments also help in monitoring and controlling maritime activity, preventing illegal crossings, smuggling, and potential terrorist threats. In essence, by strengthening infrastructure, regional countries can help ensure trade flows smoothly, while also protecting their economic and security interests. A resilient maritime infrastructure acts as a buffer against potential threats, minimising the chances of conflict escalation around this sensitive waterway.

Table (7): Investment in Maritime Infrastructure and Security Technologies (News LLU, 2025)

Investment Category	Amount Invested (USD)
Vessel Enhancements (2018-2022)	636 million
Planned Vessel Enhancements (2023-2027)	328 million
Port and Terminal Infrastructure (2018-2022)	2.1 billion
Planned Port and Terminal Infrastructure (2023-2027)	1.1 billion
Waterway Infrastructure (2018-2022)	3 billion
Planned Waterway Infrastructure (2023-2027)	1.2 billion
Integrated Maritime Connectivity and Digital Solutions Market Size (2018)	2,297.5 million
Integrated Maritime Connectivity and Digital Solutions Market Size (2022)	3,008.2 million
Integrated Maritime Connectivity and Digital Solutions Market Size (2027, projected)	3,915.0 million
Port of Los Angeles Cyber Attacks (Monthly)	40 million

Beyond just physical infrastructure, investing in training maritime patrol personnel, establishing clear communication channels, and sharing information with international partners generally enhances collective defence efforts. For Gulf countries, modern infrastructure can also facilitate a rapid response to emergencies, such as oil spills or vessel accidents, which can otherwise quickly escalate. Constructing integrated surveillance networks enables continuous monitoring, allowing authorities to quickly identify suspicious vessels or movements. These efforts not only protect vital trade routes but also uphold regional stability by deterring threats and demonstrating commitment.

Ultimately, strategic investment in maritime infrastructure acts as a shield, safeguarding economic interests while also contributing to the region's broader stability. Advancements in security technologies — including automated radar systems, long-range surveillance drones, and satellite-based monitoring platforms — open new avenues for protection, providing comprehensive coverage. These systems enable quicker detection of unauthorised vessels or unusual activity, allowing faster response times and better decision-making in this crucial maritime corridor (Ostrom et al., 2021; N/A, 2022).

8
Diplomatic Strategies and Multilateral Engagements

Regional Security Dialogues and Confidence-Building Measures

This chapter examines the intricate diplomatic plays and joint efforts influencing maritime security in the Strait of Hormuz, a key artery for global energy. Given the complex web of competing interests among regional players, multilateral platforms are becoming increasingly essential for fostering collaboration and mitigating conflict. Diplomatic efforts, particularly those involving nations such as China and India, demonstrate a growing awareness of the need to align national security goals with regional aspirations for independence and stability. China's strategic investments in ports, such as Gwadar, indicate not only economic interests but also a broader geopolitical strategy that challenges traditional Western power (Shaheen et al., 2025). Furthermore, as Asian nations increasingly acknowledge the strategic importance of the Gulf, their combined involvement might lead to a new security model that supports stability without undermining regional independence (N/A, 2022). This exploration highlights the challenges and opportunities states face in navigating a multipolar world, where multilateral diplomacy can be a crucial tool for maintaining peace and security in a contested maritime area.

The Strait of Hormuz, a vital conduit for global oil transport, has led Gulf nations to engage in regional security dialogues aimed at fostering trust and cooperation (Berkofsky et al., 2021). These discussions are crucial for addressing complex maritime issues, such as piracy, territorial disputes, and the risk of conflict, all of which are increasingly relevant in today's geopolitics (Shukri et al.). Such dialogues provide a space for countries to express concerns, exchange intelligence, and collaborate on security initiatives. The Gulf Cooperation Council (GCC) forums, for example, unite member states to address security challenges, including maritime safety. Through these avenues, nations such as Saudi Arabia, the UAE, and Oman work to harmonise their objectives and develop unified strategies against threats in the Strait. These dialogues underscore collective security and a mutual understanding of national strategies, which, in turn, prepares them for coordinated action against possible disruptions. Furthermore, numerous bilateral and multilateral dialogues have arisen, encompassing Gulf states alongside external stakeholders invested in regional stability. Nations such as the United States, the United Kingdom, and various European countries often participate in these talks, thereby promoting a broader framework for maritime security that addresses both regional and global influences (Berkofsky et al., 2021).

Collaborative Approaches to Maritime Security

Contemporary maritime security necessitates a consideration of both regional factors and the broader global implications. Such cooperation becomes essential because it acknowledges that maritime security is not a solo Act; instead, it needs collaborative efforts that respect the sovereignty and address the concerns of states within the region. At the same time, safe passage through crucial waterways must be ensured. Confidence-building measures, or CBMs, play a crucial role in enhancing maritime security within the Gulf region. These measures aim to decrease tensions and misunderstandings between nations, primarily by building transparency and promoting open communication. Establishing hotlines between naval forces, for instance, can prevent incidents at sea and facilitate immediate dialogue should unexpected encounters occur – a finding supported by studies on maritime risk reduction (Islam, 2024). Such actions help create a more predictable and secure maritime environment, and predictability is essential for the stability of the Strait of Hormuz. Multilateral initiatives further support these confidence-building efforts by bringing stakeholders together to address shared security challenges. For instance, initiatives such as joint naval exercises, information-sharing platforms, and regional security conferences foster an understanding that collaborative engagements can yield benefits for all, even while respecting national sovereignty, as discussed in analyses of international cooperation in maritime contexts (Sahakyan, M., 2024). These interactions build trust and, importantly, allow individual maritime security policies to align with collective, regional objectives. It is therefore essential for Gulf nations to carefully navigate the balance between ensuring autonomy and participating in collective security frameworks. While CBMs can certainly improve regional stability, countries must articulate their national interests and, indeed, their "red lines" to preserve their sovereignty. By fostering a security structure that incorporates both multilateral cooperation *and* respect for individual state autonomy, Gulf countries can effectively address shared maritime challenges. At the same time, they reinforce their independent decision-making capabilities. This approach contributes to regional peace and strengthens global security by ensuring the safety and security of vital shipping lanes, reflecting the interconnected nature of both regional and global maritime interests.

Role of International Organisations (e.g., IMO, UN) in the Strait

The Strait of Hormuz, a globally significant choke point for oil transit, draws considerable attention, and international bodies such as the International Maritime Organisation (IMO) and the United Nations (UN) play key roles in navigating its complex security and diplomatic landscape (Reykers Y et al., 2023). The IMO, a specialised UN agency, takes charge of regulating international shipping, crafting and enforcing safety and security standards for vessels in the Strait. It actively promotes navigational safety, endeavours to prevent pollution, and sets shipping practice regulations aimed at mitigating the risks of accidents or intentional disruptions. This is notably important considering the increasing vulnerability to cyber threats, as seen in incidents involving satellite navigation systems (Androjna A et al., 2020). The IMO's work involves developing ship routing guidelines and traffic separation schemes, and it provides security protocol recommendations for member states to enhance marine operation safety in the region.

Meanwhile, the United Nations, operating under its broader mandate to uphold peace and security, fosters diplomatic dialogue and encourages collaborative efforts among littoral states, as well as the broader international community. It fosters confidence-building by providing a platform for peacefully resolving disputes that arise in the Strait. Occasionally, incidents have been addressed through Security Council resolutions and General Assembly debates, to de-escalate tensions and preserve navigational freedom, a point of increasing importance as security challenges evolve (Reykers Y et al., 2023).

Graphic (2)

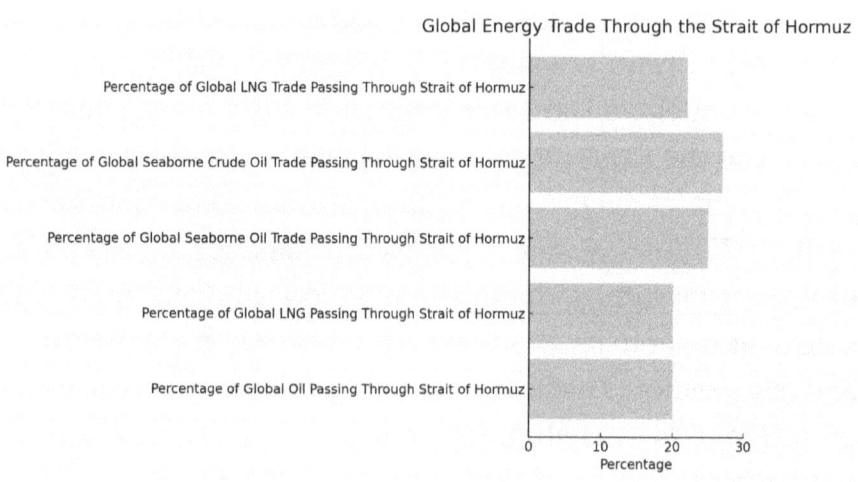

The chart illustrates the significant percentages of various global energy trades that pass through the Strait of Hormuz. It highlights that 27% of global seaborne crude oil trade and 25% of global seaborne oil trade use this passage. Additionally, both oil and liquefied natural gas (LNG) trades have substantial shares, with 20% for each. This underscores the Strait's critical role in the global energy supply chain.(Administration UEI, 2024)

Diplomacy and Maritime Security in the Strait of Hormuz

The UN framework underscores the importance of sovereign boundaries while simultaneously affirming the right of innocent passage through international straits (Sahakyan M, 2024). Alongside states bordering the Strait, regional actors find support from these organisations via technical assistance and encouragement of collaborative maritime security initiatives (Badawi, H, 2024). The balancing act between environmental concerns, commercial interests, and political sensitivities is facilitated by their combined efforts in shaping this strategic corridor. When regional tensions escalate, the role of such international bodies becomes critical, as they provide mechanisms for dialogue and negotiation that can prevent incidents from escalating into broader conflicts. However, the efforts of the International Maritime Organisation (IMO) and the UN in the Strait of Hormuz do face challenges related to the geopolitical realities. While promoting international norms and maritime safety standards, enforcement relies heavily on the cooperation of the states involved, a few of which may have competing strategic interests. The delicate balance between regional autonomy and collective security remains, as states often view international oversight with suspicion, fearing interference in internal affairs. Therefore, it can create a challenging environment for the UN and IMO to exert influence beyond diplomatic encouragement. Despite these hurdles, these organisations do adopt diplomatic strategies that combine technical regulation with mediation efforts. The IMO, for example, focuses on providing clear rules and frameworks that can be adopted with minimal political friction, thus allowing states to feel empowered in their decision-making. This pragmatic approach avoids confrontation by emphasising shared economic benefits and maritime safety, which are crucial for regional stability. On the diplomatic front, the UN encourages confidence-building through dialogue forums, such as regional consultations addressing maritime security, which facilitate discussions about safety protocols and incident responses. These efforts aim to reduce misunderstandings and foster transparency, which are critical in a region where incidents can quickly spiral. One key element has been promoting adherence to international conventions, such as UNCLOS.

Graphic (3)

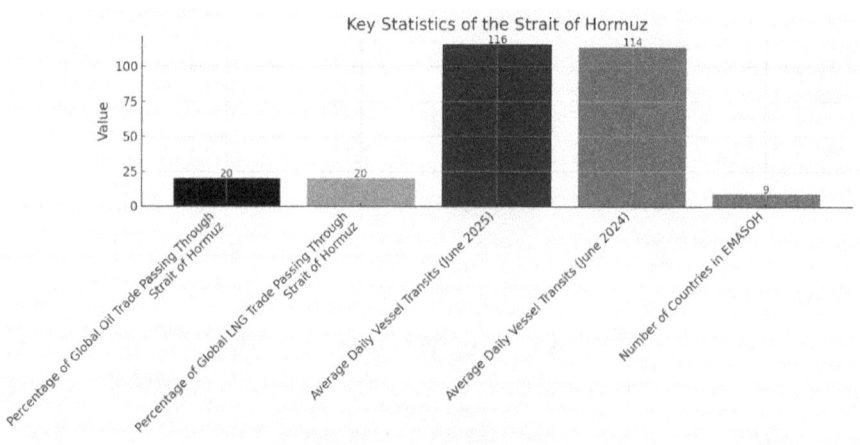

This bar chart illustrates key statistics related to the Strait of

Hormuz. It shows that 20% of the global oil and liquefied natural gas trade passes through this vital waterway. Additionally, there was an average of 116 vessel transits per day in June 2025, slightly up from 114 in June 2024. The chart also highlights that nine countries are part of the European Maritime Awareness in the Strait of Hormuz (EMASOH), reflecting international collaboration for maritime security.(Ship & Team BN, 2025)

Compliance with UNCLOS helps clarify the rights and responsibilities of coastal states and transiting vessels, thereby significantly reducing ambiguity that often leads to conflict. However, not all states in the Gulf have ratified all provisions of UNCLOS, which complicates universal application and hinders collective enforcement efforts. Furthermore, political rivalries among Gulf Cooperation Council members and between external powers often spill over into maritime interactions, challenging the effectiveness of a collective security framework that the international community is striving to establish. However, the continued involvement of the IMO and UN does generate opportunities for dialogue that might not exist otherwise, thus defusing tensions through established diplomatic channels rather than resorting to military confrontation. Recently, international organisations have also acknowledged the importance of involving non-state stakeholders, recognising that maritime security extends beyond purely state-centric approaches. By encouraging transparency in shipping operations and fostering collaboration across civil and governmental sectors, these organisations help build confidence among all parties dependent on the Strait's safe operation. Understanding the complexity, international organisations must maintain patience and a nuanced approach. Success may require reinforcing existing relationships and adapting strategies to account for the evolving geopolitical landscape.

Diplomatic Approaches to Managing Maritime Tensions

The Strait of Hormuz—a vital, narrow channel—links the Persian Gulf with the Gulf of Oman and, further out, the Arabian Sea. Around a fifth of the world's oil navigates this passage, highlighting its global importance for oil and trade (Karim A et al., 2023). Due to the number of countries that lay claim to the coastlines and waters around it, tensions about the strait's security and control frequently arise. Countries such as the United Arab Emirates, Saudi Arabia, Oman, and Iran have different interests. These nations aim to protect their access, resisting interference from others (Gábor András Papp, 2024). Such a situation presents a complex diplomatic landscape where, generally speaking, a misstep can potentially lead to serious disputes. Avoiding escalation and guaranteeing free passage involves navigating these competing claims with care through diplomacy.

Iran's approach presents a key challenge, as it typically involves using military displays and asserting sovereignty to exert control over navigation rights. When Iran views external actions as attempts to undermine its control, it sometimes raises fears of unilateral actions that could threaten safe transit. Simultaneously, Gulf states pursue assurances that their sovereignty and economic interests will be protected. External parties, such as the United States and several European countries, add yet another layer to these complex tensions, often advocating for free navigation or lending support to regional allies without direct intervention. Managing these intersecting interests effectively requires striking a balance between dialogue and assertiveness, so that sovereignty concerns do not escalate into conflict or miscalculations. When addressing regional influence, economic stability, and transit security, it becomes particularly pressing to find shared solutions. Regional cooperation, often anchored in multilateral frameworks, serves as a tool for addressing challenges in the Strait of Hormuz. The Gulf Cooperation Council (GCC), for example, has fostered dialogue among Gulf states to promote a collective approach to security. Some have recently proposed diplomatic platforms, including Iran, GCC members, and external powers, which could focus on building communication channels to avoid tense misunderstandings. In these environments, negotiation strategies typically centre on transparent information sharing, confidence-building, and joint patrols as displays of cooperation rather than confrontation. The objective is to foster trust among regional actors through agreements that reconcile security needs with respect for sovereignty. Agreements that support shared interests while respecting each nation's sovereignty, such as coast guard cooperation or joint naval exercises, have enjoyed some relative success. Outside facilitators, like the UN, or neutral actors can assist in negotiating and drafting fair and enforceable agreements. Ultimately, success depends on the integration of diplomacy with security measures to ensure that conversation leads to stability, not conflict.

9
Technological Innovations and Maritime Domain Awareness

Satellite and Aerial Reconnaissance for Maritime Surveillance

In the Strait of Hormuz, a region of vital importance to global oil transport and Gulf security, satellite and aerial reconnaissance are undeniably key to improving maritime domain awareness (Islam MS, 2024). These technologies, working in tandem, deliver real-time maritime activity data, enabling countries to monitor vessel movements, detect potentially suspicious behaviour, and respond swiftly to threats. Given the Strait's location connecting the Persian Gulf and the Gulf of Oman, it sees considerable shipping traffic, so maintaining vigilance is, of course, vital for Gulf nations. The integration of satellite imagery with aerial surveys enhances the ability to track environmental changes, monitor fisheries, and observe illegal activities, such as piracy or smuggling, which could destabilise the region (Badawi H, 2024). Analysing satellite data enables the identification of patterns in maritime traffic, facilitating predictive threat assessments. Improved satellite resolution has, furthermore, enabled the capture of detailed vessel images and the monitoring of activity, providing previously unavailable insights. Nations can, for example, distinguish between commercial and military ships, potentially easing tensions and misunderstandings. It is plain to see, in this area of geopolitical volatility, that the strategic importance of satellite and aerial reconnaissance becomes especially evident. Not only do these technologies enhance national security, but they also foster cooperation among Gulf states through shared intelligence on maritime activities that affect mutual interests. The advancement of satellite and aerial surveillance technologies presents both challenges and opportunities for Gulf nations. As nations invest, they face balancing national security interests with regional autonomy. While maintaining sovereign control over maritime security is an intense desire, the interconnectedness of threats necessitates a cooperative approach. The diverse capabilities of advanced surveillance systems might lead to varying national competence levels, possibly resulting in smaller states relying on larger ones for intelligence and support. Such a situation poses potential unequal power dynamics and could cause friction.

On the other hand, innovation provides an unprecedented opportunity for collaboration. Shared satellite systems and joint reconnaissance missions provide an opportunity for Gulf countries to enhance their defences against common threats, such as piracy and illicit trade. Establishing data-sharing frameworks can enhance situational awareness and, ideally, foster trust. The acknowledgement that maritime security affects all regional players can lead to a more unified approach. Cooperative training programs and joint exercises can further solidify collaboration. Embracing such opportunities may not only enhance security but can also pave the way for enhanced diplomatic relations in a region characterised by rivalries. To maximise these advantages, Gulf nations may consider establishing bilateral or multilateral frameworks that align their strategic interests, while also engaging in comprehensive regional security discussions (Islam MS, 2024).

Regional Cooperation for Maritime Security

A solid framework for regional cooperation can emerge through agreements that focus on sharing information and intelligence gathered from satellite and aerial reconnaissance. Stakeholders can then work together on security issues, all while maintaining the separation of national interests and their respective operations. This teamwork is increasingly based on the idea that maritime security and regional stability are interlinked, a concept reflected in current studies on Indian Ocean region security (Shaheen et al., 2025). Additionally, studies suggest that establishing these partnerships could lead to a safer maritime environment. Ultimately, this helps maintain regional stability by providing a means to quickly respond to new threats and foster trust between countries (Ostrom et al., 2021). The strategic effects of better information sharing are crucial in ensuring safety at sea and strengthening cooperative standards.

Cybersecurity in Maritime Operations

The Strait of Hormuz, a strategically important global location, handles a significant portion of the world's oil and trade. This, naturally, makes it a key area for maritime activities, but also a prime target for cyber threats (Islam MS, 2024). Ships and ports here increasingly use digital systems, which boost operations but open doors for exploitation by, for example, hackers or other hostile groups (Bergeron JH,

2021). Given the geopolitical context, cyberattacks in this region could cause disruptions that extend beyond technical issues, potentially leading to regional problems and economic consequences. Threats range from shipboard malware to interference with vessel tracking systems, such as AIS. Attacks on GPS or electronic chart systems can lead to accidents. Ports in the Strait heavily depend on connected networks linking logistics and security. Compromising these could mean unauthorised access or sabotaged operations, impacting cargo flow. These cyber risks exist along with piracy and military issues, creating complex security challenges. A significant problem is the lack of standard cybersecurity across the maritime sector in this region. While some companies may have robust security, smaller operators might still use outdated technology. The variety of actors, from fishermen to tankers, adds complexity. Cyber incidents can also, unintentionally, escalate political tensions, as attack attribution is often unclear. Digital threats have real-world strategic consequences, making cybersecurity a matter of security policy and defence (Islam MS, 2024). Awareness of these cyber risks has sparked efforts to develop tech and policy responses. Technologically, newer vessels and ports are using systems to detect abnormal activity and isolate infected parts. Enhanced encryption is protecting ship-to-shore communications, making interception more challenging. Blockchain is increasingly being used to secure cargo documents and trace the origins of shipments, thereby improving trust between parties. Satellite monitoring, combined with AI, helps spot suspicious behaviour, enhancing situational awareness.

Cybersecurity Initiatives in the Maritime Sector

To effectively manage risks that transcend national boundaries, collaborative efforts—such as shared threat intelligence exchanges and coordinated incident response teams—are crucial, as highlighted in discussions on the ethical use of technology for maritime security (Islam MS, 2024). Consider that shipping companies and port operators now face regulations requiring them to meet minimum cybersecurity benchmarks. It is also worth noting that these policies champion regular training, enabling personnel to recognise and tackle cyber threats adeptly. This essential human element emphasises the ethical dimensions of training protocols (Islam MS, 2024). For instance, the International Maritime Organisation (IMO) has issued guidelines that are being adopted by many Gulf countries, setting a baseline for both security measures and reporting practices, fostering cross-border transparency and accountability. Diplomatic engagement is indeed pivotal here: stable governance facilitates both technological adoption and regional cooperation, notably in response to evolving cyber threats. Maritime cybersecurity agreements aim to curtail misunderstandings stemming from cyber incidents, while also forging joint protocols for navigating cyber crises. Several Gulf nations have, additionally, invested in national cybersecurity centres, which vigilantly monitor maritime cyber activity and deliver real-time alerts to stakeholders, both civilian and military. However, the future of maritime cybersecurity does not solely depend on these measures. Continuous dialogue—among governments, businesses, and tech innovators—is crucial to adapt frameworks to new threats while upholding the free and safe passage of vessels, which are vital to the region's economy. This ongoing collaboration and innovation are key to staying ahead of cyber threats. It is also vital to remember that maritime cybersecurity demands constant watchfulness and adaptation, given the maritime environment's distinct challenges. Indeed, equipping crews to detect phishing attempts, consistently securing software updates, and maintaining offline backups of key navigation data can substantially bolster resilience against cyber incidents, a point aligned with concerns about technology misuse in maritime contexts (Islam MS, 2024). Let us remember that in sensitive zones like the Strait of Hormuz, even minor breaches can yield significant repercussions. Thus, layering technical defences alongside clear communication and collaboration becomes key to building resilience; comprehensive governance frameworks are thus needed to handle these issues effectively.

Data Sharing Platforms and Real-Time Monitoring Systems

In the Gulf, a region often marked by escalating geopolitical tensions, recent technological advancements have reshaped the way countries oversee and manage maritime operations. Advanced sensors, satellite systems, and data analytics offer detailed, almost real-time insights into vessel movements, maritime conditions, and cargo, thereby improving strategic oversight (Islam MS, 2024). It is essential to note that these technologies do more than help authorities identify illegal activities, such as piracy and smuggling; they are also crucial in maintaining security and preventing threats with greater efficacy. The use of Automatic Identification Systems (AIS), for instance, allows for the continuous tracking of ships, simplifying the identification of atypical activities or behaviours that stray from established navigation norms. Furthermore, artificial intelligence (AI) and machine learning algorithms are increasingly utilised to analyse extensive maritime data sets, which can reveal patterns undetectable by manual methods, thus boosting the predictive abilities of maritime operations (Gábor András Papp, 2024). The Gulf region particularly benefits from innovations such as vessel traffic management systems, undersea sensors, and drone surveillance, which collectively expand the scope of maritime monitoring and information access. These tools enhance situational awareness, enabling authorities to look beyond traditional boundaries and proactively address potential threats. Generally speaking, such technological advancements significantly enhance the precision of monitoring and accelerate response times, which are vital for protecting strategic interests in the Gulf area. Cloud platforms also play a key role by centralising data collection, which simplifies the sharing of information across agencies and streamlines coordinated responses in urgent situations, ultimately enhancing interagency collaboration.

Technological Advances in Maritime Security

The ongoing development of technology is having a significant impact on the marine environment. Here, security threats can be identified more quickly, and responses can be more precisely targeted. This progress is vital, particularly in regions with intricate geopolitical and economic setups where sea lanes are crucial for trade and fuel (Ostrom et al., 2021). For instance, data-sharing platforms in the Gulf have become crucial in coordinating maritime security efforts among various nations and agencies. The goal is to integrate data from ships, satellites, and sensors into a unified view. These platforms can display vessel locations in real-time, monitor border crossings, or alert to unusual activity. It is important to remember to respect each nation's independence. Balancing security against national independence remains a challenge. Many Gulf nations prefer to control their data, sharing specific information only with allies (Carter et al., 2020).

To solve this, systems often have access controls, encryption, and data-sharing agreements that regulate who has access to what. Look at the Gulf Cooperation Council (GCC) for joint security stuff. These platforms help share information quickly during crises, such as sea accidents or smuggling. Real-time systems also enable authorities to set up alerts, helping them make decisions quickly, while also attempting to minimise false alarms. Satellite images and predictive analysis can help identify potential threats before they escalate. Even with all this, data privacy and trust influence how freely nations share data. Finding a middle ground means building trust through clear agreements and secure technology that respects each nation while enhancing regional security. Practical steps include setting up data access rules, conducting regular drills to test the systems, and discussing data governance. As technology improves, countries may develop more advanced platforms that address both security coordination and independence concerns. It may be better to share relevant data only when needed, rather than providing complete transparency, to allow nations to maintain control while still benefiting from everyday awareness. A significant aspect is creating legal and technical structures that protect data without compromising the collaborative effort to safeguard important sea routes.

10
Crisis Management and Conflict Resolution Mechanisms

Designing Effective Incident Response Protocols

Navigating the intricacies of crisis management and conflict resolution in the Strait of Hormuz requires acknowledging the delicate balance between maritime security efforts and upholding regional autonomy. The Strait's strategic importance creates a complex situation. Competing national interests and pressing security concerns demand a comprehensive strategy. This might involve diplomatic talks, collaboration with others in the region, and leveraging technological advancements to enhance the efficiency of communication and operations for all parties involved. As noted in some recent studies, we appear to be entering a "Third Nuclear Age" (Futter et al., 2025). This brings both potential benefits and potential problems that significantly influence crisis management strategies. Different players are adopting different viewpoints based on their own security needs and ethical perspectives. Moreover, the ethical considerations surrounding maritime security technologies—such as unmanned systems and cyber capabilities—highlight the urgency for clear and strong oversight. We need frameworks that encourage sound judgment, protect human rights, and promote stability in the region (Islam MS, 2024). Policymakers can create stronger conflict resolution tools by encouraging conversations between countries and even non-governmental groups, and by considering ethical issues in security plans. This helps manage immediate risks and also strengthens the region's long-term independence and durability.

Designing Effective Incident Response Protocols

The Strait of Hormuz, a narrow waterway linking the Persian Gulf and the Arabian Sea, is undeniably a place of major strategic significance; roughly one-fifth of the world's oil supply navigates this passage (O'Hara et al., 2016). The region's geopolitical dynamics are intricate, shaped by a combination of international commerce, local political forces, and worries about security. The interests of nations bordering the Strait—Iran, Iraq, and the Gulf states, among others—frequently diverge, which can unfortunately lead to increased tensions and the potential for conflict (Kessler et al., 2021). Maritime operations in this crucial zone face various security threats, highlighting the necessity for robust incident response protocols and addressing cyber vulnerabilities.

Ensuring Security and Cooperation in the Strait of Hormuz

Securing this critical waterway presents numerous challenges, including potential terrorist actions, piracy, and military confrontations, underscoring the complex nature of maritime security (Islam MS, 2024). While foreign naval presence aims to protect shipping lanes, it can also be viewed as an infringement on sovereignty by regional actors, thus complicating the geopolitical dynamics (Karim A et al., 2023). Moreover, ecological threats, such as oil spills or accidents, underscore the need for a comprehensive response plan that addresses both ecological and security elements.

Designing effective incident protocols means carefully

balancing maritime security with respecting the autonomy of regional nations. A collaborative approach among Gulf states is vital; a unified response strengthens stability, potentially deterring aggressors and fostering mutual trust (Islam MS, 2024). A joint maritime framework could enhance information sharing and facilitate coordinated responses during crises, ultimately improving overall effectiveness. Regularly scheduled exercises are helpful in preparing for scenarios ranging from oil spills to military actions, ensuring stakeholders are well-trained and equipped.

Incorporating local plans is crucial because each state possesses unique knowledge of its waters, making local intelligence valuable during crises. Training efforts should combine regional knowledge with international best practices to foster a comprehensive understanding of individual challenges, thereby creating a stronger security environment (Karim A et al., 2023). Furthermore, maritime surveillance technology can significantly enhance situational awareness, enabling rapid threat responses while empowering local authorities to foster regional trust and collaboration. Joint actions can also discourage aggression while respecting legal frameworks governing international waters.

Diplomatic talks focused on shared interests—such as environmental protection and free passage—can reinforce ties and build confidence among Gulf states, thereby securing the Strait of Hormuz (Islam MS, 2024). Also, clear communication protocols can turn each emergency into a learning opportunity. Communities and agencies might analyse incidents to refine future responses, adapting protocols to evolving situations. Open dialogue and consistent training will lead to a more coordinated approach, ultimately ensuring safer passage through this maritime corridor.

Case Studies of Maritime Dispute Resolutions

The Gulf region, due to its strategic location and abundant hydrocarbon resources vital to the global energy sector, has been a persistent site of maritime disputes (Islam MS, 2024). Unclear boundaries, overlapping continental shelf claims, and the control of key shipping lanes—particularly the Strait of Hormuz, a crucial choke point for much of the world's oil—are frequent sources of conflict (Chadha A, 2023). These disagreements typically revolve around EEZs and territorial seas, as defined by UNCLOS, offering a legal basis for maritime jurisdiction (Islam MS, 2024).

Countries such as Saudi Arabia, Iran, the UAE, and Kuwait have encountered substantial obstacles in defining their maritime borders, reflecting both historical practices and contemporary legal norms. Naturally, varying national agendas make negotiations more difficult (Chadha A, 2023). Although international legal structures, such as UNCLOS or ITLOS, have been explored, political factors and varying interpretations of maritime rights have often limited their effectiveness in resolving disputes (Islam MS, 2024). A notable instance is the overlapping claims of Saudi Arabia and Iran in sections of the Persian Gulf, which, given the Strategic Importance of the Strait of Hormuz, highlights the complexities of their maritime relationship (Chadha A, 2023).

Impact of Political Dynamics on Gulf Maritime Disputes

Rights are asserted by parties over islands and water routes, shaping the command of navigation and the resources contained therein (Islam MS, 2024). The Gulf nations have at times looked to international entities to mediate disputes; however, political factors often shift conflicts toward direct talks rather than formal legal resolutions (Sahakyan M, 2024). Iraq and Kuwait, for instance, have contentious maritime borders in areas rich in offshore oil, but these disagreements also underscore broader geopolitical and security considerations, complicating straightforward legal decisions. Despite the availability of international law as a framework, diplomacy and regional accords often play a crucial role, alongside formal adjudication, in the Gulf's conflict resolution efforts. The Gulf Cooperation Council (GCC) member states have endeavoured to ease tensions by forging shared frameworks for maritime security and the management of resources for many years. While these endeavours have certainly faced obstacles, they demonstrate a leaning towards dialogue and mutual settlements instead of litigation, particularly given the possible strategic and economic effects of protracted disputes. Diplomatic solutions often prove more fruitful in this setting, where neighbouring countries balance competing interests amidst an environment of continuing collaboration and close ties. While the international system remains relevant, it serves more as background than as a definitive route to resolution. Lessons from these instances suggest that clearly defined legal boundaries, coupled with sustained diplomatic efforts, are crucial for de-escalating tensions. This strategy acknowledges sovereign claims while fostering shared use of maritime areas.

A notable example is the maritime boundary agreement between Bahrain and Qatar, which specifically defined territorial waters and jurisdiction over particular islands. While the matter escalated at times, both sides presented their case to the International Court of Justice (ICJ) in 2001. In the same year, the court made a ruling, affirming maritime boundaries and sovereignty. Consequently, both nations were able to progress with their resource development plans. This occurrence demonstrates the potentially constructive function of legal bodies when both parties recognise their jurisdiction, also accentuating the significance of persistence and negotiation before resorting to legal action. In such scenarios, international law proves most effective when combined with political determination, thereby fostering opportunities for peaceful coexistence and resource sharing among Gulf nations. Looking beyond the Gulf region, we can see valuable insights from successful approaches to managing maritime conflicts. For instance, in the South China Sea, multiple claimant states have managed to sustain dialogue through the Declaration on the Conduct of Parties (DOC), established between ASEAN and China in 2002 (Islam MS, 2024). Although the debates continue, the DOC has created a forum for communication and the prevention of crises. Likewise, settlements of maritime zone disputes in the Eastern Mediterranean have been achieved via direct negotiations aided by international players (Sahakyan M, 2024).

These examples suggest that arbitration and multilateral frameworks can aid in transforming disputes into manageable problems, provided that political figures remain committed to non-violent resolutions. Closer to the Gulf, the Red Sea has a history of maritime conflicts resolved via diplomacy. After years of tension over maritime borders tied to offshore oil, Saudi Arabia and Eritrea reached agreements, supported by the United Nations, to demarcate their respective zones. Their achievements are often credited to the engagement of neutral international monitors and the careful balancing of economic benefits with security considerations. The lessons gleaned from these instances have particular importance for the Strait of Hormuz, a crucial channel for the world's energy provisions.

Preventive Diplomacy and De-escalation Strategies

In the busy waters of the Strait of Hormuz, a key transit point for global oil, preventive diplomacy is crucial for mitigating the risk of conflict (Gama IDA et al., 2021). Consider the situation when tensions arise between Iran, the UAE, or Oman: diplomatic efforts to prevent escalation can significantly help avoid a major conflict with far-reaching consequences. These efforts often involve maintaining open lines of communication, utilising early warning systems, and building confidence to demonstrate everyone's commitment to maintaining stability. For instance, the Gulf Cooperation Council sometimes tries to help out by talking to its members and keeping tensions down (T O N et al., 2021).

Building trust is key here. With trust, countries feel more at ease about sharing their concerns without fearing that someone will stir up trouble. Regular naval visits, joint train-

THE MARITIME SECURITY DILEMMA IN THE... 111

ing exercises, or meetings can foster understanding and enhance regional stability. Neutral helpers, such as the UN or regional groups, can also enhance trust and ensure that talks remain productive. Many experts stress the importance of being open and predictable in how ships move around, as it reduces misunderstandings and accidental conflicts. We have seen cases of miscommunication during naval encounters, so we recognise the need for clear rules and diplomatic methods to de-escalate situations quickly if necessary. Preventive diplomacy can also involve developing shared maritime security plans. These deals establish standard rules for being at sea, thereby reducing the likelihood of mistakes or aggressive moves. This may involve discussing maritime safety, search and rescue cooperation, and the exchange of information. Such ideas foster a sense of regional ownership over security, making cooperation a greater focus than fighting. Especially as things continue to change in the region, it remains vital to maintain those diplomatic lines open and continue talking and working together.

Graphic (4)

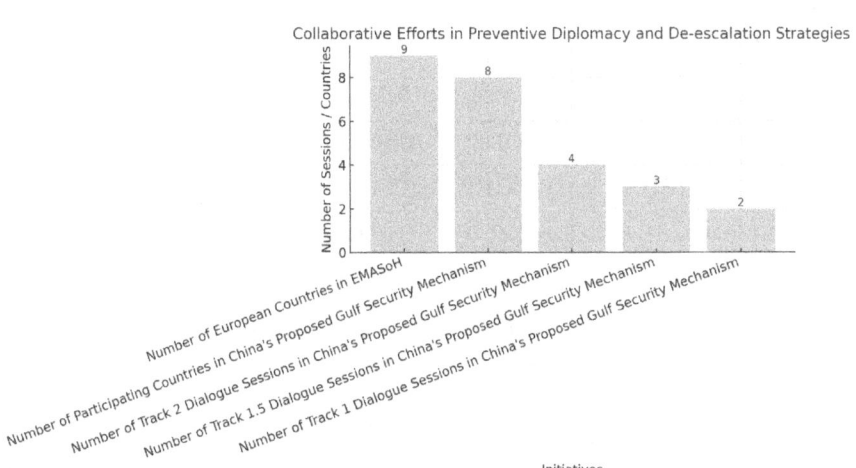

The chart displays the number of countries and dialogue sessions related to collaborative efforts in preventive diplomacy and security in the Strait of Hormuz. It shows that nine European countries participate in the EMASoH initiative, while eight countries engage in China's proposed Gulf Security mechanism. The dialogue sessions vary, with four Track 2, three Track 1.5, and two Track 1 sessions established as part of this mechanism.

Regional Conflict Management and Security

Building trust through ongoing dialogue is crucial for preventing incidents that could escalate into larger conflicts (Islam, MS, 2024). Strategies for de-escalation play a vital role in managing conflict while respecting the independence of each nation. This balance calls for strategies that reassure countries about their safety without encouraging aggressive behaviour. Often, diplomatic efforts focus on building mutual interests, such as securing shipping lanes or collaborating to counter piracy (Selth, 2022). Joint patrols, hotlines, or shared intelligence can help establish a sense of partnership, which might ease tensions. These measures show a mutual desire for stability, making conflict less desirable. Formal negotiations or mediation by a third party are essential tools in conflict resolution. When tensions rise, dialogue can be facilitated by credible mediators or regional forums that allow for expression and remedies.

Consensus-building requires patience and an understanding of each state's security concerns and regional interests.

For instance, negotiators might draft agreements that outline clear rules, specify dispute resolution procedures, or establish joint committees to monitor compliance. Flexibility is key, as firm positions tend to deepen distrust and complicate dialogue. Keeping communication lines open during crises helps prevent misunderstandings from escalating into violence. Balancing security with regional independence involves acknowledging each country's interests while promoting collective security and stability. Ensuring that security arrangements do not infringe on sovereignty fosters broader participation and commitment. Knowing that all parties are considered in decisions fosters a sense of shared responsibility. This includes regional security agreements that respect national borders, as opposed to unilateral actions that heighten local tensions. Multilateral agreements on maritime patrols or early warning systems can serve as confidence builders, laying the groundwork for lasting peace in the region. Transparency and respect for sovereignty are important when implementing these strategies. Clear communication, inclusive processes, and patience can help ensure that de-escalation efforts are maintained. As tensions escalate, the emphasis should remain on building mechanisms that facilitate dialogue and peaceful resolution, rather than escalation or confrontation. Practical steps, such as establishing communication lines or minimising military aggression during sensitive periods, can significantly reduce the risk of accidental conflict, particularly in a region as strategic as the Strait of Hormuz.

11
Building Regional Security Architectures

Multilateral Security Frameworks and Alliances

The Strait of Hormuz, a narrow yet vital waterway connecting the Persian Gulf and the Arabian Sea, is of immense importance; approximately 20% of the world's oil passes through it. This fact alone underscores its significance to global energy security (N/A, 2022). Bordered by countries such as Iran, the United Arab Emirates, and Oman, regional security is understandably a complex issue, further complicated by differing political objectives and long-standing rivalries. Disruptions to this crucial choke point can have substantial implications for international trade and oil prices; indeed, the stakes extend beyond those nations directly bordering the strait to impact the entire global economy (N/A). Consequently, addressing the numerous challenges presented by this unique geopolitical environment requires a close examination of evolving security cooperation and alliances among regional actors. Generally speaking, understanding these dynamics is crucial to international security.

Strategic Security in the Strait of Hormuz

The economy's dependence on oil transported through these waters highlights the region's strategic importance in global energy supply chains (N/A, 2022). This area often sees tensions due to political conflicts, military activities, and foreign naval forces, which can escalate quickly because of the high geopolitical stakes (N/A). Countries like Iran utilise their geography to assert influence, making it necessary for regional partners to coordinate security efforts to mitigate these tensions. The security landscape is thus complex, with differing views on military presence and intervention leading to potential friction among allies. The unique security needs of Gulf states have led to various alliances and agreements that reflect these dynamics. Nations must address both external threats, such as piracy and terrorism, and internal political dynamics that impact regional stability. Competition for regional influence complicates relationships further, making it crucial for Gulf states to navigate partnerships to promote shared interests carefully. Adequate security measures must strike a balance between national interests and collaborative efforts to maintain regional peace and stability. A multifaceted approach, encompassing military readiness and diplomacy, is vital for effectively addressing regional security challenges. Ultimately, understanding the Strait of Hormuz's strategic landscape is crucial to grasping the significance of multilateral security frameworks, as they lay the groundwork for regional cooperation. Understanding how nations forge alliances, balance national interests, and confront common threats enhances the ability to navigate future challenges. Building cooperation among Gulf states, while respecting each nation's preferences, fosters stability and security in this volatile region. Engaging stakeholders, from government to civil society, can further enhance efforts to secure the strait and broader region, ensuring a collective approach to shared vulnerabilities.

Joint Maritime Patrols and Intelligence Sharing

The Strait of Hormuz stands as a strategically vital waterway, serving as a choke point through which approximately 20% of the world's daily oil supply passes (N/A, 2022). Given its economic and geopolitical weight (N/A), securing this narrow passage—less than 40 miles across at its most constricted point—has been a long-standing priority for Gulf nations. Collective efforts such as joint maritime patrols in the area are intended to maintain security, deter piracy, and prevent illicit activities, such as smuggling and unauthorised military movements. These patrols are not just about ensuring safe passage for commercial vessels; they also visibly demonstrate cooperation between neighbouring countries concerned with the stability of this crucial maritime corridor. However, these joint patrols encounter challenges, most notably from geopolitical tensions and the need to balance competing national interests. Regional countries, generally speaking, have differing views regarding which forces should participate and the operational frameworks. For example, trust issues, often present between Gulf nations and external powers with a naval presence, complicate the creation of sustained, unified command structures. The narrow confines of the Strait, coupled with heavy traffic from both civilian and military vessels, add to the coordination complexities. Clear communication and shared engagement rules are essential to prevent incidents that could escalate. Geography itself poses challenges to joint maritime patrols in most cases. Patrol ships face limited manoeuvring space due to the Strait's small size and shallow depths, which heightens the risk of accidents, particularly considering the region's high strategic significance (N/A, 2022).

Intelligence Sharing in Maritime Security

Sandstorms pose a challenge to effective surveillance; consequently, nations rely on a combination of methods—surface ships, aerial patrols, and, increasingly, maritime drones—to achieve comprehensive monitoring (N/A, 2022). The aim? To protect the movement of goods and promote shared awareness, which should hopefully boost trust in the long run. Intelligence sharing is vital, particularly in a zone like the Strait of Hormuz, where the volatile nature of threats is amplified by its critical role in global energy. Although Gulf countries grapple with piracy and the threat of terrorism, political considerations and other issues tend to complicate cooperation in intelligence exchange. States must carefully weigh the advantages of working together against safeguarding their own sovereignty, which often translates to a deliberate approach when sharing sensitive data. Even so, the desire to prevent incidents has encouraged both formal and informal intelligence-sharing arrangements, creating safer maritime activities. Naval units and coast guards share data on potentially dangerous vessels, enabling swifter action and better awareness in a challenging environment. Liaison officers and secure lines between neighbouring countries ensure streamlined information flow, securing sensitive information while strengthening collective security. These methods try to balance the protection of information with engaging in collective security, bit by bit establishing trust between the participants (N/A).

External parties with a naval presence have a significant influence on regional balancing efforts, shaping the strategic thinking of countries involved. Partnerships with global naval forces unlock advanced technologies and assets, but also raise concerns about reliance on outside help (N/A, 2022). For nations navigating this complex network, transparency and solid agreements are essential for fostering trust. Effective intelligence sharing can enhance operations and reduce potential misunderstandings, which is crucial during a crisis. Joint patrols, despite their advantages for security, come with their own political difficulties, mirroring the broader regional situation that cannot be ignored. Building trust requires continuous dialogue, transparency, and mutual respect—all vital components of any long-lasting security structure. Initiatives such as shared maritime coordination centres and standard protocols are steps towards formalising cooperation. To that end, policymakers should encourage focused intelligence exchanges that could lead to more comprehensive partnerships; a gradual approach helps test existing cooperative efforts, developing respect and understanding without unnecessary exposure.

Developing Regional Maritime Command Structures

The Strait of Hormuz, a narrow waterway, is crucial for global energy, particularly oil supplies. A substantial percentage of the world's oil—approximately 20% of all globally traded oil—passes through this vital choke point, underscoring its significance to regional security and international markets

(Ostrom et al., 2021). Control over the Strait, in most cases, directly influences global oil prices and their availability, making it a key area of concern for countries seeking stability and access. Disruptions here, it should be noted, can have far-reaching impacts, affecting not only economies but also political relationships far beyond the immediate area (Faculty of the Department of Affairs NS et al., 1998). Therefore, the Strait of Hormuz remains a pivotal area in geopolitical discussions related to energy security and, more broadly, maritime strategy.

Strategic Significance of the Strait of Hormuz

The Strait of Hormuz's significance is not *just* about energy. It is also deeply entwined with maritime trade, the regional balance of power, and diplomatic ties between Gulf states, Iran, and the wider world (Brewster et al., 2014). Tensions there can, and do, cause wild swings in oil prices and even imperil global economic stability (Kumara et al., 2021). Thus, regional and global players are keenly aware of the delicate balance required to protect this vital passage. However, safeguarding the Strait? That is no easy feat. Political friction among Gulf countries, especially Iran's positions and relationships, complicates things (Brewster et al., 2014).

Acts of interference, such as attempted blockades or maritime harassment, periodically put the stability of the Strait of Hormuz at risk. The geography itself presents a challenge; narrow channels and heavy traffic make surveillance and patrols difficult. Non-state actors, piracy, and smuggling further complicate security operations. Despite technological advancements, maintaining a reliable presence in the waterway remains a challenging task, necessitating coordinated actions from regional allies and international partners, with clear plans in place for emergencies (Kumara et al., 2021). A robust security solution requires genuine cooperation across the region, combining military readiness with diplomatic talks. While individual countries have their own naval strengths, no single nation can fully secure such a vital waterway on its own (Brewster et al., 2014). A practical framework would involve sharing intelligence, conducting joint patrols, and establishing clear communication lines to prevent incidents from escalating. Building trust among the Gulf Cooperation Council (GCC) states, Iran, and other relevant parties is crucial. This involves respecting sovereignty and ensuring that security measures are perceived as a shared responsibility, not an imposition. Implementing this collective security system requires careful consideration. Countries must agree on who does what, how, and have response protocols that are clear and accepted. Regular joint exercises can improve coordination, and diplomatic channels must stay open to resolve disputes before they escalate. International bodies, such as the International Maritime Organisation, can support this effort by providing guidance and facilitating dialogue.

The ultimate goal is to strike a balance where regional countries maintain control over their waters while collectively addressing threats, embracing new technologies, and ensuring that security measures do not impede free navigation, which is crucial for global trade. Looking ahead, the focus needs to be on creating security arrangements that are both flexible and robust. This could involve regional maritime patrol units, shared intelligence networks, and joint incident response teams. Stressing transparency and diplomacy helps avoid misunderstandings and reduces the likelihood of miscalculations. Practical steps could include establishing clear communication protocols, sharing real-time information, and conducting regular joint training sessions. As maritime security evolves, maintaining an adaptable and trust-based approach among regional partners is crucial for protecting the Strait of Hormuz and ensuring the safe passage of international shipping (Brewster et al., 2014).

Maritime Security and Sovereignty

The concept of maritime security has gained momentum, providing a means to align security measures better while respecting each country's sovereignty (Ezeh KD et al., 2023). These setups aim to facilitate easier naval intelligence gathering and sharing, enhance coordination among patrols, and respond to threats promptly without compromising national interests. The concept suggests that maritime security is a concern that affects us all, but it must be handled with care, respecting each state's autonomy to manage its own affairs. Setting up command centres or joint teams often means establishing rules that outline how decisions are made and where each group can operate, ensuring that no single group dominates or contradicts the country's objectives. Many regional projects focus on establishing patrol networks, either through shared command centres or agreements between two countries. Countries might use their own ships, but they communicate with each other through a central communication hub. This helps share information, cuts down on repeating tasks, and makes everyone more aware of what is going on. For instance, consider military teamwork in the Gulf Cooperation Council (GCC), where joint exercises and data sharing are effective ways to work towards a unified maritime approach (Vo HQ et al., 2023). Still, each country's wish to maintain control over its waters must align with the need to collaborate—demonstrating how trust and respect are essential in these partnerships. Building strong command setups also means having clear job assignments and knowing who is responsible for what. Countries must agree on the main goals, such as stopping piracy, patrolling the seas, and providing assistance in emergencies. Rules for talking, sorting out conflicts, and handling crises are essential to avoid mix-ups or accidental misunderstandings. Regular joint drills and tests can help check these systems, enabling countries to become more comfortable and confident with each other.

Additionally, involving regional groups—such as the Gulf Cooperation Council or other similar organisations—can lend legitimacy, facilitate coordination, and help resolve disagreements. Ensuring each state's autonomy is respected helps more countries participate and strengthens the partnerships necessary for long-term maritime security. Lastly, new technologies such as shared watch systems, satellite tracking, and tools to monitor activities at sea should be integrated into the command setup. These help with real-time intel and faster choices. As regional maritime command systems evolve, maintaining an open and transparent approach to communication remains crucial. Countries need to adhere to a Plan that respects each country's sovereignty while offering opportunities for collaboration. The aim is to create a network that can evolve, is trusted by everyone, and can handle new threats without compromising regional freedom or alienating important players. This even-handed approach is vital as maritime challenges become more complex in the years ahead.

12
Practical Strategies for Balancing Security and Autonomy

Policy Recommendations for Sovereignty Preservation

The Strait of Hormuz, through which approximately 20% of global crude oil transits, constitutes a pivotal intersection of economic and strategic dynamics for both the region and the international community. Its constricted geography inexorably alkalises the wealth and geopolitical heft of the waterway, thereby attracting a spectrum of foreign stakeholders. The fundamental challenge is safeguarding the Strait's routes without infringing on the constitutional boundaries and prestige of the Gulf Cooperation Council (GCC) states.

Stationing extramural maritime assets ostensibly confers a layer of protection on commercial and naval traffic; yet, the attendant operational footprint can, at times, obscure the territorial autonomy conferred by international law upon the littoral states. The reality is a membrane of trust wherein the transit security of the Strait is rhetorically international, yet the operational and legal locus remains Gulf-centred. Hence, fundamental to the security discourse is deliberate calibration: the GCC must negotiate strategic assurances that exclude extraneous agendas and transform protection into Gulf-centred schemes that, at a minimum, prevent the licensing of foreign vessels that port in Saudi, Emirati, or Omani territorial waters.

Pragmatic examination of military and diplomatic instruments is required to protect regional stability without encroaching on the prerogatives of the Gulf states themselves. A policy portfolio is therefore needed that simultaneously defends international security objectives and sustains the sovereignty of the partner states. One viable element of such a policy is to devise a security architecture that restrains external postures while energising intraregional cooperation and establishing a basis for coordinated prosecutorial initiatives.

The proposed architectural component would facilitate a periodic dialogue on transboundary hazards and foster a locus of stakeholder ownership. In parallel, the system should expand diplomatic circuitries with extra-regional actors, such that the operational footprint in the Strait of Hormuz is codified within a framework that affirms Emirati prerogatives and guarantees the uninterrupted transit of commercial shipping. Gulf interlocutors, therefore, should frame incipient accords to juxtapose navigational permission with the non-precedent of sovereign forfeiture.

The provenance of satellite monitoring technologies can supplement situational awareness, providing a light-footprint and less stressful deployment alternative to expansive external basing. Lastly, substantive linkage with multilateral bodies can furnish quasi-forum endorsement, permitting regionally endorsed expeditionary actions while visibly centring Gulf-derived authority in the operating command. Collectively consolidated, such steps would enable the sovereign articulation of regional utility while remaining a discrete and organic component of broader maritime stability initiatives.

Establishing mutually supportive Gulf maritime security partnerships would furnish a protective layer against emerging threats, while simultaneously cultivating trust and collaboration among regional maritime actors. A systematic approach to professional exchanges and resource sharing can build indigenous operational capacity, allowing Gulf countries to assume custodial responsibility for their own waters and decrease dependence on external military presences. Such a pathway fortifies a stable but sovereign posture, safeguarding national interests and simultaneously meeting collective security requirements in the Strait of Hormuz without subordinating decision-making to extra-regional powers.

Operational Tactics for Threat Deterrence While Respecting Autonomy

The Strait of Hormuz, as the preeminent artery for global oil shipments and regional economic viability, presents a persistent security focal point and demands a calibrated security presence. Any effort to institute persistent surveillance and presence in the Strait must be meticulously calibrated to deter potential hostile vectors while avoiding provocation of the Iranian military and paramilitary layers. A predetermined, bracketing rotation of maritime formations—conducted solely within the twelve-nautical-mile seaward limit of the Strait—should be shared with coastal states in advance, reinforcing joint schematic legitimacy and minimising the perception of hostile or intrusive motives.

Joint patrolling arrangements—hosting observers from regional Gulf nations—foster confidence rather than cultivate mistrust. They counter unilateral demonstrations of force that frequently heighten regional anxiety and compromise local governance. Equally consequential is the calibrated distribution and intensity of naval assets in the operational theatre.

Employing the less provocative capabilities of patrol boats or surveillance drones enables forces to convey a posture of deterrence while remaining within politically acceptable limits. Such capabilities significantly reduce the risk of being misunderstood, a common issue that can arise when deploying larger combatants. At the same time, these lighter platforms retain the agility to interdict illicit cargo or respond to navigational hazards, thereby establishing a persistent surveillance backdrop without appearing coercive.

Cooperation with domestic coast-guard units augments these initiatives. Local personnel possess context-specific knowledge that enhances situational awareness, while their participation lends domestic legitimacy to the broader maritime security arrangements. Complementing this interoperable approach is the institution of secure, regular communication networks that link naval contingents, local authorities, and commercial stakeholders. Advance notification of patrol sequence and operational intent serves to demystify presence and diminish the potential for operational friction.

Transparency serves as both an instrument of effective operations and a foundation of political repose. When maritime, aerial, and surface patrols adopt an open-architecture posture and complement that stance with regular exchanges across national and institutional hierarchies, they mitigate the destabilising effects that abrupt autonomous troop movements might impose upon the already fragile security equilibrium of the Strait. A substantive strengthening of security collaboration across the Gulf requires mechanisms that enable states to share relevant information and cultivate behavioural assurance without infringing on sovereign prerogatives.

Frequent, inclusive multilateral meetings provide arenas within which grievances can be articulated transparently and misapprehensions can be rectified before they crystallise procedurally and strategically. Such congregations can be expanded to include civilian diplomats, scholarly practitioners, and relevant representatives of the maritime commercial community, thereby broadening the nexus of mutual regard and advancing comprehensive security discourses. Confidence-building measures emerge as pivotal instruments for alleviating tensions between neighbouring states that carry intricate and sensitive legacies.

Exemplarily, a consensually established protocol requiring prior notification of major naval and aerial exercises, or the mutual interchange of Automatic Identification System (AIS) and radar track data, diminishes the apprehension surrounding sudden manoeuvres and delineates the normative pattern for foreseeable behaviour. When states consciously participate as equal participants in the formulation and review of these measures, a solidified perception of reciprocity and esteem ensues. Such a shared obligation precipitates a

THE MARITIME SECURITY DILEMMA IN THE... 133

non-competitive disposition, displacing adversarial extrapolations, whilst incontrovertibly sustaining the sovereign latitude of each polity to exert decisions consonant with its own strategic imperative.

Trust cannot be bequeathed but instead cultivated in the soil of small, consecutive actions, and this is particularly true where the soil is marred by long-standing geopolitical acrimony. To that end, practical exercises such as synchronised maritime search-and-rescue drills or recurring, joint humanitarian deployments in the same estuaries and cities are low-cost, low-risk ways to generate habitual, observable cooperation. Because these tasks hinge on material, calculable gains—saving lives and ensuring the flow of regional sea-lanes—operational commanders on all sides can endorse them without suspending the prerogative of making independent national choices. Common purpose can therefore emerge without any formal or rhetorical recoil from autonomy.

Once practical cooperation becomes habitual, the meticulous habit of acting together can, with domestic and regional market needs, evolve into deeper security arrangements rooted in a shared sentiment of mutual security rather than in historical stipulations of rank. A decisive approach to persuading policymakers to endorse these activities is to articulate them, both publicly and privately, as collaborative, mutual stabilisation investments rather than as transactional minimisation of security easing restrictions. When pitched in this manner, the projects signal to circumspect capitals that the joint arrangements will siphon the regional gains of security and clearance to discouragement before any external capital's interest is felt. The framing also primes the capitals to frame the resulting stabilisation as a consequence rather than as acquiescence.

The effect is to permit every participant to sustain domestic legitimacy while taking measured diplomatic risk, a mode of calculated hedging that is indispensable in the politically and culturally delicate theatre of the Gulf, where reputational thresholds for bargains exceed material terms and can materialise with subtlety, slower than verbal.

Countries bordering the Strait of Hormuz have consistently recognised the waterway as indispensable to the uninterrupted flow of global energy and the broader regional economy. Oman and the United Arab Emirates have each pursued strategies that safeguard those interests while preserving a degree of political and operational autonomy—complementary devices rather than identical instruments. Oman's approach leans heavily on striking a balance between diplomatic cultivation and the selective maintenance of military readiness. The Sultanate's long-standing policy of neutrality allows for an expansive and nuanced relationship with the principal external powers. At the same time, a small, focused naval component underpins a presence sufficient to signal authority without alarming potential adversaries. Oman's diplomatic apparatus, through quiet but persistent mediation, helps curb the escalation of regional flashpoints and simultaneously ensures the unimpeded transit of civilian and commercial shipping.

Contrast that with the Emirates, whose posture is unequivocally proactive and, occasionally, overtly declarative. Abundant investment in a technologically sophisticated naval arm—complemented by a pronounced reliance on the co-production of advanced military systems and systematic joint training—results in a combat-ready, agile maritime complement. Western military partnerships, most conspicuously with the United States, are not subordinate amenities but fused components of the overall operational calculus. Destined not merely to meet an autonomy criterion, these collaborations confer economies of scale, intelligence-sharing synergies, and immediate augmentation potential. Simultaneously, the Emirates' substantive participation in branded regional initiatives—multilateral maritime security dialogues and coordinated mixed-force patrols—has lent its naval posture an appeal to collective rather than unilateral defence, mitigating the sting of possible suspicion while accentuating deterrence.

This blended strategy allows the state to safeguard its economic assets while overtly refraining from encroaching on neighbouring sovereignty, as it commonly justifies operations in the light of wider regional stability. Parallel to this, the two nations have adopted economic manoeuvres to enhance security. Oman negotiates the uninterrupted export of oil and secures key passage rights through judicious diplomatic engagement. Its deliberately elastic policy facilitates recalibration in response to evolving regional conditions while avoiding firm entrenchment in rivalries. The United Arab Emirates, by contrast, capitalises on its pioneering maritime assets by positioning its supply and logistics platforms as vital security anchors, thereby conferring concurrent economic and strategic advantage. These disparate instruments portray how Gulf states, while differing in operational nuances, pursue a singular, overriding purpose: the defence of the crucial waterway, all within bounds of sovereign autonomy and recognised regional responsibility.

The efficacy of these nation-specific tools ultimately hinges upon seamless cooperation with extra-regional allies. Omani tradition of impartial diplomacy, reinforced by a lengthy reputation for confidentiality, frequently casts it in the role of unobtrusive intermediary, capable of hosting negotiating conclaves and moderating dialogue between polarised factions. The Emirati nexus of military alliances, in contrast, provides auxiliary assurance through supplementary frameworks, particularly in recurring exercises and cooperative intelligence dissemination.

The synthesis of diplomatic engagement and military readiness produces a stratified security architecture that curtails the likelihood of hostilities while preserving national independence. The examined cases illustrate a guiding tenet: the equilibrium between protection and self-governance is contingent upon well-articulated strategic ends and policy elasticity. Oman operationalises this doctrine through an unwavering stance of non-alignment and a diplomatic-first posture, thereby functioning as an anchor of equilibrium within the Peninsula.

The United Arab Emirates, in contrast, illustrates that a forward security stance, when complemented by intentional partnerships, reinforces collective aspirations without generating over-reliance upon nominal patrons. Both polities evidently confirm the feasibility of preserving national volition in an unstable theatre when the policy architecture

THE MARITIME SECURITY DILEMMA IN THE... 137

is underwritten by meticulous foresight, systematic confidence-building, and a nuanced perception of the prevailing strategic milieu. Constructive diplomacy, consequently, has been the pivotal variable in sustaining an ordered maritime environment in the Strait of Hormuz.

Individual states have therefore pursued inclusive pacts that foreground the free passage of vessels and concomitant risk-reduction assurances. The Council's initiatives, for instance, institutionalise a framework for periodic security dialogue to mitigate friction and foster a sense of communal accountability. Such platforms, in the aggregate, permit collective Gulf agency while affording each member the latitude of inviolable governance rights.

Amid periodic escalations in the Gulf region, diplomatic engagement serves as the primary mechanism for de-escalation, effectively diverting states from resorting to unilateral actions that could compromise national sovereignty. Alongside diplomatic initiatives, sustained military cooperation plays a crucial role in sustaining a stable security environment. The converging interests of Gulf states in securing unobstructed transit through the Strait have prompted coordinated efforts, such as joint maritime patrols and reciprocal coast-guard accords.

Such initiatives mitigate the risk of miscalculation and reduce the likelihood of unintended hostilities. The provision of training, intelligence sharing, and tailored technological assistance by the United States to selected Gulf states, for instance, reinforces national defensive capacities while allowing partner governments to retain authority over security doctrine and decision-making.

Complementing these bilateral undertakings, regional and extra-regional multilateral institutions have conceived regular forums designed to facilitate transparent discussion and confidence-building measures. Recurrent maritime exercises, in turn, enhance joint operational effectiveness and serve as tangible indicators of concerted resolve. The International Maritime Exercise (IMX), conducted annually and encompassing both Gulf navies and Western maritime forces, epitomises this approach by projecting a coordinated stance while meticulously respecting the sovereignty of each participating state.

Such multilateral undertakings reaffirm the understanding that collective security does not entail the forfeiture of sovereign discretion; rather, it enlarges the individual state's capability to address dangers while the choice of policy remains domestic. These instruments achieve their highest efficacy only where cooperative arrangements are based on transparency and confidence. The Gulf states acknowledge that reliance solely upon military capabilities can produce unwanted escalation; therefore, the infusion of diplomatically mediated collective endeavours offers reassurances that security instruments possess a defensive, rather than a hostile, character.

Among the principal benefits is the promotion of broader regional engagement, which retains the liberated room for manoeuvre of individual states while easing the overall strategic environment. The arrangement's symmetry allows states to adjust to novel challenges rapidly without compro-

THE MARITIME SECURITY DILEMMA IN THE... 139

mising their sovereign prerogatives. Strengthened defensive posturing is complemented by intensified regional economic interconnectedness, which in turn functions as a subtle form of non-kinetic influence.

Joint commitments to infrastructural ventures—such as the development of shared maritime and telecommunications facilities—generate a web of mutual dependence that diminishes the likelihood of armed confrontation. When the perceivable gain of maintained tranquillity outdistances the cost of strategic confrontation, collaborative diplomacy acquires priority. The schemes hence become instructive demonstrations of the compatibility of state security and state discretion when diplomatic, rather than coercive, instruments prevail.

The principal conclusion is that sustained security is best secured through deliberate transparency, reciprocal respect, and practical alliances that reinforce rather than compromise sovereign authority. A review of the Gulf states shows that enduring order hinges as much on the quality of diplomatic practice as on the breadth of deterrent capability. When states strategically calibrate their diplomatic and security postures to align with regional and global standards, they can safeguard their vital interests without yielding dominant control over domestic structures.

13
Future Trends and Emerging Challenges

Impacts of Climate Change and Environmental Factors

Climate change is rapidly emerging as a significant source of security risk within the maritime domain, exerting mounting pressures on narrow yet strategically vital choke points, such as the Strait of Hormuz. The urgency of this issue is underscored by the fact that the Strait serves as a conduit for an estimated one-third of the oil traded internationally. Elevated sea levels, compounded by a notable intensification of meteorological variability, are progressively altering the operational geometry available to vessels transiting through the area.

A perceptible increase in the density and severity of storm events now constitutes a persistent hazard, heightening the likelihood of groundings, collisions, and cargo loss, thereby compelling the denial of sea lanes upon which diversified, interlinked regional economies depend. Concurrently, average sea temperatures have transposed key trophic regimes, shifting the distribution of commercially vital pelagic stocks and elevating tensions—often multilayered—over long-standing and, in some instances, unresolved fishing jurisdictions.

These cumulative trends detrimentally intersect the projected operational tempo of both naval and maritime commerce, compelling a strategic recalibration. The need for this recalibration is crucial, as defence algorithms, shipping risk profiles, and marine navigational doctrine are now implicitly obliged to assimilate climate-induced variability to restore, to some extent, the regional stability that, by legacy, is the aegis of constancy noted by contemporary states.

Increasing sea temperatures may drive marine organisms to redistribute, compelling states to recalibrate their strategic doctrines governing resource stewardship and maritime security. However, this redistribution also presents an opportunity for regional cooperation, imposing an imperative of agility on naval forces. This potential for collaboration, especially in the face of evolving environmental norms, can foster a sense of hope and optimism among the audience. Concurrently, prevailing geopolitical relations within the Gulf are increasingly influenced by the delicate balance of regional ecosystems, rendering deeper cooperative mechanisms indispensable for the equitable and sustainable use of the shared marine basin.

This cooperative imperative transcends the resolution of pressing, short-term disputes and instead cultivates enduring adaptive capacity in the face of the accelerating effects of climate change. Environmentally driven challenges undermine the premises of long-standing geostrategic scripts; consequently, states whose littoral borders encompass the Strait of Hormuz are compelled to reconcile their security postures with demonstrably meaningful sustainability objectives in harmony. Such recalibration is no longer auxiliary to the geopolitical agenda, but central to preserving the region's strategic integrity over the longer term.

Temperature differentials, modified oceanic currents, and

attendant shifts in salinity and stratification will progressively convert shipping routes into zones of heightened vulnerability, thereby recalibrating the calculus of energy security. Melting cryospheric extents, which are areas of the Earth where water is in solid form, have cascading effects on salinity balance and circulation, whose reverberations are manifested in altered naval manoeuvre envelopes and potentially disrupted maritime arteries. A systemic appreciation of the nexus between environment and maritime security may yield policy directives capable of simultaneously sustaining effective governance and prudent resource stewardship.

For instance, countries in the region could realise substantial dividends by channelling resources into environmental resilience initiatives designed to pre-emptively counter climate-related disturbances, thereby reinforcing national security while nurturing valuable regional diplomatic ties.

Emerging nontraditional Security Threats (e.g., Cyber, Climate)

The Gulf, distinguished by its vital maritime corridors and pre-eminent economic weight, is increasingly confronted by non-conventional security hazards extending well beyond state-on-state military confrontation. Cyber threats and climate dynamics are among the foremost challenges, each introducing multifaceted vulnerabilities to maritime stability. Cyber assaults directed at maritime logistics or port facilities jeopardise the uninterrupted transit of commerce, to which the Gulf is inextricably attached. These incidents can incapacitate navigational systems, postpone the arrival of consignments, and, in more dire scenarios, catalyse sizeable downstream economic damage if pivotal digital infrastructures are breached. The exposure level is further aggravated by the constant progressive integration of digital systems into vessel tracking, offshore energy operations, and port oversight procedures. Simultaneously, climate change is re-shaping the Gulf's environmental baseline, thereby generating secondary friction at the maritime security interface. Elevated air and sea temperatures, shifting mean sea levels, and the increasing regularity of acute weather phenomena exert mounting stress on coastal facilities and military assets alike. Notably, elevated sea surface temperatures may lead to a statistically significant increase in the intensity of storm activity, thereby endangering the integrity of vessels and coastal facilities.

Prolonged onshore water scarcity, induced by recurrent drought episodes, channels demographic pressure through labour migration and transboundary absorption, indirectly feeding the insecurity calculus of adjacent polities. Simultaneously, the retreat of polar ice, although geographically remote, creates expanded Arctic transit corridors that are poised to recalibrate long-standing patterns of global shipping, potentially altering the Persian Gulf's foundational position in the maritime supply chain. Together, these converging pressures invariably ensnare response architectures in heightened complexity.

From another perspective, succeeding climatic catastrophes—hurricanes, floods, and heat-stressing waves—generate cascading disruptions across information and transportation sectors, granting cyber aggressors a broader exploitation horizon. Physical vulnerabilities in ports, tank farms, and undersea cables, altogether heightened by systematic under-maintenance and climatic fatigue, amplify the deterrence calculus of sovereign fleets and commercial operators alike. No maritime actor retains the jurisdictional or technical singularity necessary to insulate itself; therefore, the coordinated assimilation of situational awareness and rapid recovery protocols has evolved from aspirational to essential.

The confluence of these challenges predetermines that contemporary strategy must negotiate the narrow interstice between exercising state sovereignty and undergirding collective security. Correspondingly, several Gulf polities have advanced elements of a long-range resilience schema, whereby layered cyber defences are engineered to safeguard backbone systems integral to navigational and energy-export activities. Executives emphasise three interrelated thrusts: creating isolated, encrypted communication architectures; forwarding intelligence-gathering systems to cyber defence technicians; and instilling simulation-based curricula that advance incident management tempo on the hardened defensive perimeter.

Systematised sharing of threat intelligence among Gulf states offers a proactive defence against emerging risks that could disrupt port and hydrocarbon terminal activities. Early warnings derived from maritime surveillance or cyber indicators can diminish the likelihood of attacks that, left unattended, could immobilise strategic national facilities. Concurrently, climate-related vulnerabilities, marked by rising sea levels and intensified storms, compel collective rather than solely national action, as ecological boundaries are inherently porous. In this context, intensified collaboration among the Gulf monarchies has recently led to initiatives for advanced meteorological forecasting and coordinated stockpiling of emergency recovery assets, thereby enhancing the region's overall climate resilience.

Parallel diplomatic initiatives focus on integrating environmental shock-absorption strategies into the more conventional security frameworks that govern naval exercises and maritime patrol planning. Such embedding is intended to counter the assumption that environmental and security agendas are wholly discrete, emphasising the interfacing of infrastructure protection and ecological integrity. These multitrack endeavours thereby strive to preserve the necessary equilibrium between sovereign prerogative and cooperative compact, for states inevitably seek to advance their own prosperity. At the same time, cognisant that unilateral gestures can generate exposure. Regional forums, notably the Peninsula Shield and the Gulf Cooperation Council's security subcommittees, thus provide neutral platforms whereby states can calibrate their security objectives without irrevocably alienating decision flexibility.

Trust, in this dynamic, is reinforced not only through bold rhetoric but also by the systemic use of shared training exercises, personnel exchanges, and secure communications drills—all of which create shared experiences that lower the temperature of suspicion and render the prospect of collaboration calculably safer. Over successive cycles, occupant strategic narratives concerning adversarial spirals have gradually accommodated the legitimacy that national planners now attribute to nontraditional transnational risk, gradually broadening the security aperture to encompass not only the kinetic threat to infrastructure but also the kinetic and non-kinetic dimensions of resilience itself.

Such systematic experimentation produces a framework that can likewise be extrapolated to any oceanic region confronting a similar nexus of vulnerabilities. A disciplined understanding of how digital intrusion and climate stressors intersect enables strategic decision-makers to align defence capital and diplomatic bandwidth with pressing estuary needs. Upgraded maritime security architecture no longer equates solely to the presence of naval and aerial forces; equal if not pre-eminent investment must be diverted towards fortifying cyber architectures and designing systems that can dynamically endure shifts in oceanic and atmospheric conditions.

Cross-portfolio consultation among defence ministries, oceanic stewardship agencies, and technology incubators imposes reflexive discipline and iterative re-evaluation on strategy, rendering responses agile across a spectrum of future latent dangers. The particular complement of vulnerabilities already encountered on the Gulf seaboard may provide transferable heuristics for sustaining seawall security amid a world marked by polycentric, asymmetric interdependencies.

The swift incorporation of advanced information technology is adjudging traditional maritime security theories in paramount regions, a case in point being the Hormuz corridor. Constellations of low-Earth orbit optical and synthetic aperture radar, unmanned surface and aerial vessels, and hyperspectral and multispectral passive sensors provide governments and multilateral agencies with unprecedented granularity of maritime situational awareness, thereby compressing decision cycles. These capabilities allow operators to delineate and catalogue vessel signatures, extrapolate threat-node probability webs, and implement prompt countermeasures against violations of sovereignty, including piracy and strategic embargo circumvention.

These technological advancements compel regional actors to reevaluate how to reconcile national decision-making autonomy with the obligations arising from collective security arrangements. Sustaining domestic surveillance capabilities invites friction over the governance of data collection regimes, access protocols, and the diffusion of intelligence, friction that may, in turn, be transmitted into broader deterrence and assurance calculations. The Strait of Hormuz, owing to its pronounced geostrategic significance, epitomises this negotiation; the same suite of radars, drones, and persistent over-the-horizon sensors can, under asymmetric or asymmetrical use, function either as a stabilising deterrent or as a triggering pretext for unwanted escalation. The dualism of these emerging systems—protective when national and regulatory boundaries are observed, yet perilous when data outcomes are misallocated or misinterpreted—renders governance a matter of grave geo-economic and security significance.

Second-order emerging technological issues are compounding the Strait's stature as the region's technological fulcrum. The cyber domain, in particular, poses a threat to the very algorithms, messages, and status arrays that generate maritime domain awareness. Misalignment or hostile-directed cyber probes against automatic identification systems, satellite data relays, or national coastal surveillance servers may cascade into a multiple-episode malfunction, where vessel tracks are distorted, entire shipping lanes are retrofitted with false signals, or signalling misalignment occurs, resulting in rigid national responses that generate entry bans. The result can be fused; erroneous vessel categorisations precipitate calculations of hostility, and misrouting algorithms divert tankers towards tighter transit arcs, precipitating the maritime Latent Trigger called 'collision by effectiveness'. The domain of cyberspace is the most critical and the most stealthy, challenging regional actors to internalise equally lopsided security measures, and that permit the same algorithms to be embodied in both defensive posture and in the technical deterrent that deters adjoining states. Creators use the intelligence derived from labelled maritime activity.

UAV configurations—including autonomous aerial vehicles and uncrewed surface vessels—are progressively redefining how maritime operations are conceived and executed. Although their employment may enhance situational awareness and expand the reach of maritime response functions, they remain vulnerable to cyber and electromagnetic attacks that could disseminate false information or divert mission-critical efforts. Such susceptibility raises broader concerns about regional sovereignty, particularly in instances where coastal states are developing indigenous unmanned capabilities to enforce maritime claims independently, thereby recalibrating traditional power dynamics.

Preserving maritime stability in an environment that highlights these emerging technical vulnerabilities requires deliberative strategies and constructive multilateral engagement, despite the universal imperative to foster proprietary technological superiority. Growing dependency on an advanced lattice of sensor, communication, and processing systems compels an equally thorough appraisal of their operational constraints and threat vectors. For illustrative purposes, the substitution of terrestrial or aerial sensor cues by satellite-based imagery and tracking leaves any degradation of satellite continuity—either via legitimate denial techniques or covert cyber insertion—capable of generating significant surveillance voids in otherwise monitored sea lanes.

Furthermore, unmanned entities are designed to execute missions over operational envelopes that are prone to external perturbation—including dynamic meteorological phenomena, persistent and fluctuating electromagnetic interference, and predictable denial actions by an adversary—thereby limiting mission reliability and reproducible performance in the operational theatre. Regional security constructs, hence, are obligated to embody redundant systems architectures and cascading mission back-ups to distribute probative credit across heterogeneous sensors and decision circuits. Concurrently, the safeguarding of national uncrewed operations and depot support systems must, as a priority, be consolidated along the space of sound cyber doctrine and clean tier architecture, to preclude systemic commandeering or malign latencies introduced into mission decision loops by unfriendly entities.

The accelerating pace of technological advancement necessitates the intentional incorporation of resilience into the design of maritime security frameworks. Constructive measures could encompass the establishment of regionally integrated surveillance networks that interconnect adjacent maritime nations, coupled with the systematic exchange of threat intelligence. Such steps would mitigate latent vulnerabilities and enhance the efficacy and speed of collaborative response mechanisms.

14
Policy Recommendations and Implementation Frameworks

Developing Comprehensive National Maritime Security Strategies

As the principal conduit for oil shipments connecting the Persian Gulf to the Arabian Sea, the Strait of Hormuz—with a minimum width of 21 nautical miles—serves a strategic function of disproportionate global significance. Consequently, the protection of the Strait is a national imperative for any economy whose stability or growth depends on Gulf-origin hydrocarbons. However, protection efforts must be conducted in accordance with the established principles of national sovereignty exercised by the Gulf States themselves.

A maritime security strategy, therefore, must proceed from the premise of regional autonomy, which, in practice, entails careful reconciliation of several often-conflicting imperatives. It is advisable to engage, on a prioritised basis, the full spectrum of Gulf governance—from hedging navies through local fishermen cooperatives—so that prospective security measures may be informed by tacit knowledge of maritime usage, customary jurisdictional boundaries, and the varied socio-economic logics that underpin local ordering. These social and political matrices are the only way to establish equilibria that are credible for the purpose of stabilising the Strait for international commercial purposes.

Engaging the stakeholder community generates strategies tailored to the realities of the Gulf environment, thereby reducing the potential for external, game-changing intrusions and creating a shared baseline of trust among cooperating countries. A sufficiently robust strategy should explicitly call for coordinated drills and the symmetric exchange of intelligence, thereby permitting sovereign states to confront maritime hazards collectively without encroaching upon each other's decision-making hierarchies. National maritime resilience in the Gulf, therefore, requires the design of policy architectures that accommodate the distinct imperatives of each member while advancing the shared goal of sub-regional cohesion.

Establishing a Gulf coalition for maritime security presents a well-founded mechanism for amplifying normative cohesion. Such a mechanism could standardise situational awareness protocols, optimise the sequencing of maritime patrol tasks, and systematise contingency responses to in-progress events. The coalition, to achieve internal legitimacy, should overlay national task forces with softly hurled institutional architectures that include common operational pools and phased integration of hardware. Consonant with maintaining the operational sovereignty of participating states, the coalition's constitutional code would permit temperate adaptation of national helicopters, uncrewed patrol vessels, and volunteer hospital vessels in a training theatre agreeable to all. Periodic war-gaming exercises, which provide realism through hypothetical contingencies such as hijacking, cyber-initiated dereliction, or stealth infiltration, will offer a controlled laboratory for adaptive learning in advancing states' path dependence toward effective collectivity.

Developing a regional digital platform for communication

and information sharing among Gulf states will significantly enhance real-time situational awareness and facilitate swift, coordinated responses to emerging maritime challenges. The simultaneous integration of advanced maritime surveillance capabilities—satellite-based tracking complemented by AI-driven data synthesis—will deliver synchronised, informed decision cycles across the peninsula and extend protective coverage to the entire Gulf milieu. Proposals emerging from this initiative, therefore, must remain actionable and focus explicitly on cultivating a diplomatic environment favouring dialogue and partnership rather than confrontation.

Regular, institutionalised dialogue with external stakeholders, underpinned by accession to maritime treaties of regional and global relevance, is likewise essential for consolidating trust and maritime security across the Gulf's contiguous waters. Strategic doctrines must retain sufficient flexibility to adjust to the swiftly evolving global security landscape while remaining firmly anchored in the geopolitical and cultural realities of the Gulf.

The Strait of Hormuz occupies a central and historic locus in the geopolitical configuration of the Gulf basin. For centuries, its confined waters have functioned as a crucial conduit for global energy shipments, rendering the security of this narrow passage a collective imperative for all Gulf littoral states. Successive generations of Gulf decision-makers have comprehended the direct correlation between economic prosperity and the safeguarding of unimpeded navigation through the Strait, making cooperative security a longstanding imperative in regional maritime policy.

Geographically clustering states are subject to reciprocal pulls that can nominally outweigh ideological variance, encouraging them to weigh the advantages of concerted governance against the costs of discord. Should armed friction erupt, the externalities immediately radiate outward: the Strait, as a narrow international highway, serves the downstream energy transactions of states that do not border the Gulf, linking exporters, refineries, and major markets to a singular, uninterrupted logistical cadence. Consequently, delay and hazard to the waterway transform apprehension into a region-wide indeterminate risk, prompting a loose but durable consensus on the desirability of a minimum deterrent threshold. This tacit norm periodically crystallises into coordinated initiative.

In episodes of acute diplomatic strain, several Gulf capitals have instituted combined naval sweeps, reciprocal signal exchange networks, and joint risk assessment desks to mitigate hazards that, while transitory, could metastasise into systemic disorder—as was the case with episodic piracy and transiting contraband trade. The attitudinal foundations of such operations remain tentative, to be continually reinforced through practical dividends: every arrest, every queried vessel that does not evolve into a boarding, decreases the individual national insurance premium on vessels and cargo. The strategic calculus that binds them, therefore, forswears treating the Strait as a battleground for raw coercive leverage, recasting it instead as the channel through which Gulf consumers, Gulf importers, and, indeed, Gulf citizens remain bound to the larger, fluctuating rhythm of the global economy.

Gulf security dynamics around the Strait of Hormuz demonstrate a recurring divergence between national rivalries and inevitable self-restraint exercised by all major stakeholders; the sea lane's economic multiplier effect consistently eclipses the ephemeral attractiveness of military escalation. Strategic interlocutors, therefore, seek formal and informal diplomatic dialogues, even as more extensive regional dissensions remain frozen. Historical observation establishes the Strait as a perpetual cooperative lodestar capable of absorbing otherwise regional animosities, reminding that the core calculus of economic interdependence can constitute a significant brake on conflict escalation.

The preservation of an interlocutory and imminently shared custodianship of the Strait is, therefore, indispensable for preempting an outbreak that would otherwise roll back economic and political security in the broader Gulf area and ripple into continental economies beyond. Reconstituting regional confidence thus turns on the definition and institutionalisation of mutually intelligible and operationally credible security routines, rather than the rhetorical invocation of bilateral privilege. Confidence-building must commence from reciprocal transparency, operationally intensified by the phased adoption of multilateral maritime workshops, and, over successive cycles, trilateral and quadrilateral naval tactical exercises, which disclose operational intent, refine formal communication protocols, and cultivate a common appreciation of expanding regional norms.

Seepage of divergent operational assumptions is, in effect, the pre-correction of lethal ambiguities. Supplementary protocols for routine information exchange would encompass not only routine shipping lanes and scheduling, but also custom check-on-check threat assessments, aiming to establish overlapping warning zones and aligned retaliatory thresholds that prevent accidental tactical escalation. A regional maritime domain awareness observatory, in which representative national and coalition maritime information cells collect, correlate, and publicly disseminate unobtrusive and agreed-upon indicia of both everyday sea commerce and differentiated threat emissions, would constitute an institutional platform capable of testing and, as required, intensifying regionally accepted preventive action.

To institutionalise collaboration, riparian states could establish a binding code of conduct for the Strait of Hormuz. Such instruments would articulate detailed engagement protocols to govern crises, privileging diplomatic resolution over coercive measures. Proxy guidance for inter-ship communications, submitted for reciprocal ratification, could magnify anticipatory signal clarity and so curtail unintentional hostilities.

Durable observance, however, hinges on an authentically negotiated text that captures and balances distinctive risk perceptions, thereby securing reciprocal accommodation and limiting future disputes over interpretation. In parallel, a systematic integration of civilian and naval constituencies is advisable within confidence-building programmes. Periodic exchanges involving port authorities, data sharing among regional mariners, and coordinated vessel movement notifications would enhance normative habituation and crystallise a shared operational lexicon.

Regional joint task forces, charged with combating cross-border irregularities such as syndicate-led human trafficking, unlawful fishing, and logistics chain sabotage, can foster routine inter-service cooperation. Such mundane, outcome-oriented cooperations accentuate a platform of reciprocal dependence, cultivate low-visibility inter-agency rapport, and supersede an over-preoccupation with traditional rivalry. Acceptance of an interoperable horizon of sovereign prosperity, anchored on a stable Strait, would gradually ration an erstwhile competitive mindset in favour of a redistribution and functional arrangement of responsibility.

Promoting structured dialogue forums at both state and societal levels cultivates a durable reservoir of mutual trust. Leveraging diplomatic efforts, underpinned by carefully maintained communication channels, diminishes the space within which misunderstandings flourish and enables familiarity to develop. When incremental trust is fostered through persistent and transparent exchanges, the prospect for progressively bolder arrangements in maritime cooperative security materialises while the likelihood of conflict escalation is correspondingly reduced.

Sustained dialogue provides a forum for the ongoing calibration of cooperative initiatives in response to emerging developments, thereby ensuring action remains adaptable in the face of shifting maritime patterns around the Strait while safeguarding fundamental regional priorities. Practitioners aiming to solidify regional collaboration along strategic seaways should prioritise low-tension, confidence-generating initiatives, such as instituting direct and secure naval communication hotlines or convening regular maritime security seminars that engage a spectrum of stakeholders. Such deliberate, incremental measures establish a robust precedent that simplifies the management of future, more complex political or military divergences.

Monitoring and Adaptive Management of Security Frameworks

The construction of effective monitoring regimes for the Strait of Hormuz security framework necessitates the specification of precise, quantifiable performance criteria. Suggested criteria encompass incident recurrence rates, latency intervals for incident management, or the extent of cooperative actions among regional stakeholders. Systematic reporting cycles and analytical frameworks enable national ministries, security services, and partner jurisdictions to discern successes and to institute timely corrective adjustments.

It remains essential to draw a precise line between centralised oversight and respect for sovereign autonomy when designing containment frameworks. To that end, any monitoring architecture must operate in tandem with national policies, producing utility for the collective security community without encroaching upon territorial prerogatives. One pragmatic solution is the establishment of multilateral, encrypted intelligence-sharing nodes that can cross-check anomalous patterns while not encroaching on any single nation's data space, thereby balancing rigour and restraint.

Operationalising such frameworks requires a three-pronged approach. Surveillance must be underwritten by unassailable transparency, complemented by calibrated accountability thresholds and dynamic, iterative feedback loops that transpose empirical outcomes into iterative blueprint cycles. Alongside statutorily mandated adjustments, a dual architecture that interfaces cutting-edge technology with seasoned human supervision is indispensable. High-resolution satellite sweeps, persistent maritime reconnaissance, and layered big-data analytics converge to provide timely indications that guide human assessment towards potential irregularities.

Complementarity is further achieved when coalition members subscribe to a federated data architecture that aggregates parameterised risk indicators, with role-restricted, rights-managed apertures calibrated upon national levels of contribution. Concurrently, capacity building that equips personnel to scrutinise data, transition into predictive modelling, and rehearse decision-stream choreography is pivotal for minimising interpretative leakage. Lastly, the system architecture must be architectonically porous, enabling the injection of refreshed indicators, upticked deemed patterns in asymmetries, or emergent operational tempo without inducing cycles that outlast the emerging tempo itself.

Systematic audits supplemented by independent external assessments substantially bolster the credibility of security initiatives and promote enduring trust among the diverse range of stakeholders. By calibrating the interval and scope of such examinations, one can reinforce the principle that strategic monitoring does not entail encroachment on sovereign prerogatives, thus cultivating a cooperative climate while safeguarding jurisdictional autonomy. Circumstances surrounding the Strait of Hormuz, marked by heterogeneous security traditions, validate that prescriptive doctrines are invariably counterproductive.

Dynamic strategic frameworks permit authorities to recalibrate, rather than rigidly implement, broad policy contours by processing real-time situational data. Continuous horizon-scanning of both regional and extra-regional indicators—emerging military capabilities, modified alliance architectures, or escalated diplomatic tensions—underpins a proactive rather than reactive posture. Illustratively, a sharp surge in maritime piracy statistics may prompt an immediate reallocation of resources to stand-off maritime patrols, while concurrently advocating for harmonised domestic legal frameworks to expedite prosecution.

Progress in diplomatic tracks or the introduction of restrictive measures in one or more member states may necessitate a reassessment of cooperative modalities, potentially requiring statutes of limitation or adjustments to data-sharing regimes. Flexibility and durability are ensured by fixed review intervals, binding stakeholders to systematic assessments of milestones and recalibrated action deadlines. By regular instead of ad hoc reconciliation, the policy apparatus averts obsolescence and preserves a continuous, calibrated response to emergent or imminent threats, thus strengthening overall security coherence.

Successful adaptation also requires that all stakeholders maintain substantive, continuous lines of communication. The timely distribution of intelligence and situational analysis generates an up-to-the-minute common operating picture, supporting rapid, coordinated action as new threats arise. Accordingly, decisive, well-rehearsed procedures for concluding decision cycles should be articulated and ready for immediate activation whenever an unforeseen risk materialises.

Scenario-driven strategic exercises to construct a catalogue of possible stress events enable governments to chart and refine an array of pre-authorised, adaptable response pathways. For example, should diplomatic friction rise sharply, a structured progression of countermeasures—ranging from back-channel talks to phased military re-posturing—can be set in motion without delay. A deliberate, persistent culture of mutual trust and situational candour is therefore indispensable, so that partners perceive necessary policy recalibrations as legitimate rather than destabilising surprises.

When sovereign states and key regional stakeholders jointly draft these frameworks, the resultant documents are more than paper accords; they become common property, sparking a voluntary sense of inclusion that curtails the friction that typically accompanies unilateral adaptation. The disengaged observer thus finds reinforced fidelity to the norms and an increased capacity for timely modification as external circumstances evolve.

15
Conclusion and Path Forward

Synthesising Key Insights and Lessons Learned

The Strait of Hormuz remains the world's preeminent maritime bottleneck, linking the Persian Gulf to the Gulf of Oman and the Arabian Sea and facilitating the transit of roughly one-fifth of the global crude intake. Its elevated salience to international energy and security architectures elicits continual scrutiny, particularly against the backdrop of fluctuating oil dependency and regional contestation. The mutual entanglement of self-assertive national projects, hierarchy-driven power configurations, and persistent external contestation animates the surrounding geopolitical environment.

Iran, the United Arab Emirates, and Saudi Arabia share overlapping yet diverging stakes in safeguarding the Strait and its residual governance. The consequences of maritime disruption for the basin's security and the world's economy are stark—predatory delays, sinkings, or mines can elevate crude pricing within hours, transmitting inflationary shockwaves from Gulf component economies to energy-hungry consuming markets. Nor is collateral damage confined to energy transfers; supply chain re-routing and maritime insurance recalibrations amplify monetary market, banking, and securities dynamics in reciprocal economies.

Comprehensive shocks that escalate toward a prospective blockade or flash conflict would precipitate adverse consequences, ranging from West African oil ports to Taiwanese semiconductor supply, due to intricate economic linkages. Strategic observance of the Strait hence attracts multidimensional international actors, for whom sustaining maritime constancy has become a relatively low-cost compensatory security imperative. The concomitant presence of carrier battle groups and submarine-hunter facilities further immunises external principles from the perennial re-negotiation of Gulf political authority by indirectly reallocating deterrent resoluteness. In turn, the arena's intra-basin polities face salience attenuation of sovereign option structures to the extent that coercive equilibria between the United States, Russia, and selective Euro-Asian arenas deny or condition Gulf choice.

A further imperative is the cultivation of strategic flexibility within the conduct of foreign policy. Gulf monarchies must continually calibrate their partnerships with diverse global powers, remaining flexible enough to uphold their sovereign interests. Achieving this equilibrium typically entails a triad of sustained diplomatic outreach, calibrated economic reciprocity, and a readiness to adjust certain stances in the interest of broader benefit.

Polities exhibiting this dexterity invariably accrue a proportionate currency of influence, being able to mitigate the contingency of superordinate players. Beyond relying on entrenched patrons, the deliberate expansion of multidimensional economic linkages serves to both amplify autonomy and dilute the leverage of any singular power. A complementary avenue lies in deepening domestic consultation through broader civic forums. Marginal and mainstream stakeholders, including opposition elements and civil societal institutions, should be integrally involved in the practices of dialogue surrounding standard security, shared governance, and dispute resolution.

Such a constituency-based paradigm could yield widely shared and legitimate outcomes while progressively fostering reciprocity, thereby steadily reducing entrenched distrust. By introspectively examining the chronicles of past crises and augmenting the mechanisms of collaborative security planning, Gulf regimes can cultivate a resilient framework of reference to absorb the perennial uncertainties associated with the Strait of Hormuz and its environs.

Strategic Recommendations for Policymakers and Stakeholders

The Strait of Hormuz is indisputably the most consequential choke point in the global energy supply system. Approximately 20 per cent of world petroleum shipments traverse its narrow channel, cementing its role as the primary conduit for shipments, particularly for the Gulf Cooperation Council (GCC) states. This waterway's importance, however, transcends economics; it embodies profound geopolitical sensitivity.

The dense intersection of regional security dilemmas with global market imperatives inflates its prominence, intensifying rivalries over surveillance, policing, and the symbolic question of sovereignty. The Strait's restricted depth and the proximity of archipelagos and harbours consolidate the Strait as a focal point for maritime militarisation and political coercion. The symbolic struggle for sovereignty over what amounts to a submerged border encapsulates broader regional power contestations.

Historically, foreign militaries have maintained varying levels of deployment to guarantee unimpeded transit and prevent wider systemic economic dislocation. However, such presences frequently intersect and, at times, conflict with the GCC's objective of maritime autonomy and, by extension, regional dignity. The enduring friction between the assertion of Persian Gulf sovereignty and the qualitative necessity of overseas security guarantees, if left unmitigated, is likely to mutate into an open diplomatic or possibly kinetic crisis.

The Gulf equilibrium will remain stalemated as strategic mini-crises feed on miscalibrated external and intra-responses. One pole possesses geographic dominance: Iranian adherence to brokerage zones and past, as well as selective and sharp congestion, illustrates the leverage of ebb-and-flow control. Opposing these intermittent pressures, permanently deployed international naval groups serve as rotating deterrents; yet, their presence, itself an object of contention, complicates cooperation, shifting calculations daily within and beyond Gulf capitals.

In the overarching security architecture, the Strait of Hormuz emerges as a double-edged sword: both a scar from past accelerations and an axial emblem of proliferating mutual stakes. Fluctuations in thread sizes, even brief, stress the structural cost of militarised presence and punctuate the ceilings on assured continuity. Between lies thin tissue— exertion of minimal, yet unequivocal naval presence to protect thoracic shipping and restraint against self-fulfilling signalling escalation. Navigate, still shifting.

Mediating the Strait through outside steady-state frameworks invites scrutiny of intra-Gulf hinge populations. Proportional assessment of state-level reactive vectors, calibration of cooperative readiness, and herding of security aggrandisement aspirations collectively delimit autonomy. Concurrently, aspirant local control postures encounter the circulating logic of global economic dependencies, revisited substitution lists, and barrel-by-barrel pennant flows. Arranging, recalibrating, appreciating, if incurred, the revocations of elevated security, one narrow latitude of strategic exclusion affects, quickly, all latitude lines.

Policymakers are urged to design maritime security initiatives that reinforce safety in the Gulf while safeguarding the sovereignty of the coastal states. Approaching security measures in a calibrated manner enables the mitigation of tangible threats without creating a climate of dependence or suspicion. Precedents demonstrate that frameworks based on shared responsibility outperform bilateral or dominant unilateral alternatives in delivering durable confidence.

The littoral states retain the geographical, economic, and operational primacy required to secure the Strait of Hormuz. Coordinated measures—particularly integrated maritime surveillance, periodic joint patrols, and streamlined intelligence sharing—would capitalise on this primacy. Establishing robust, encrypted communications to pre-notify maritime movements and incidents can thereby limit the risk of miscalculation. Such initiatives should be regularly reviewed in diplomatic channels to maintain strategic coherence.

Opening an inclusive convocation to candidly discuss piracy, maritime smuggling, and threats to offshore infrastructure can harmonise perceptions and reinforce deterrents based solely on collective needs. Third states, in turn, should be invited to contribute complementary capabilities—such as surveillance, training, and medical evacuation—through a lens of restraint that deliberately avoids conspicuous force projection. Consolidated dialogue, convened by the Gulf Cooperation Council and optionally by neutral maritime authorities, would establish a habitual and credible channel for continuous calibration and the peaceful resolution of emerging disputes.

This multilateral framework fosters gradual and pragmatic advance without surrendering the autonomy of individual states. Fundamental to effective policymaking is the simultaneous recognition of the sovereign rights of the Gulf states and the unavoidable reality of their shared responsibility for the security of vital waterways. The appropriate balance can be institutionalised through scheduled joint exercises, the adoption of common navigation and operational safety standards, and the drafting of interoperable contingency plans.

Forward-looking policies must develop the capacity to withstand emergent dangers—such as cyber intrusions or violent extremism—that threaten liberty of navigation with minimal escalation in defensive postures. The persistent, predictable, and candid nature of political and professional exchanges is the best empirical barrier to the kinds of trust deficits that invite strategic instability, particularly in the confined channels of the Strait of Hormuz. One promising avenue for stakeholders thus entails the creation of non-proprietary maritime domain awareness architectures, which utilise existing satellite, radar, and Automatic Identification System (AIS) feeds.

Collecting and sharing this information in near real-time can mitigate the chances of misrecognition, shorten reaction times, and produce a shared operational picture that, by design, is more rigorous than any single flag officer might otherwise produce alone. When aggregated, these discrete interventions create a maritime environment that is secure, enduring, and aligned with the development objectives of all Gulf states, thereby serving as a force multiplier for sustained stability and prosperity in the region.

Building Resilience: A Long-term Vision for the Strait of Hormuz

The Strait of Hormuz remains indispensable for global energy security: nearly one-third of the planet's exported oil traverses its twelve-mile corridor. Even momentary stoppages catalyse rapid ripple effects, elevating pump prices, altering cargo routing, and shifting calibrated balance sheets worldwide. For riparian and adjacent Gulf states, averting disruption is therefore less a matter of projecting national power than of guaranteeing the ongoing stability of their own fiscal lifelines.

Stability can be secured only by recognising the intrinsic interconnectedness of the challenges presented, which span national, sectarian, and technological seams. Long-term resilience cannot be stamped into existence; its sinews are woven through a systematically structured strategy. Planners, therefore, are obliged to anticipate the spectrum of political, military, and existential hazards and design structural solutions immune to the fleeting logic of coercive, unilateral deterrent behaviour. Such designs, resilient by discipline, acccpt the dynamism of technology and power and couple emergent national incentives to sequential global opportunities for collective action.

The health condition of the Strait's waters affects the credibility of state institutions that host its banks, its energy ports, and its national security architecture. Corrective meticulousness at its institutions is essential, yet no single polity can absorb and deflect the cumulatively asymmetric pressures of its imperial and parochial neighbours; only a durable institutional architecture anchored by deliberative regional coordination can systematically repulse systemic thresholds. Given the persistence of asymmetrical relationships, parochial grievances, and the normative acquisition of peer geopolitics, a shared security calibre forged, calibrated and vetted individually yet collectively, is the only attainable sovereign currency.

The fundamental task is to harmonise the divergent prerogatives of the Gulf states while steering clear of conflict escalation. A durable vision will be anchored in the modernisation of infrastructure that strengthens economic autonomy and enhances defensive capacity. Equally, genuine resilience can flourish only when institutions embed it within the social contract—through comprehensive education, active civic participation, and accountable governance.

If the policy lens encompasses quarters rather than quorums, Gulf polities can envisage a typical horizon in which enduring stability is a collective asset, conferring latitude upon the coalition rather than upon the individual. Strengthening resilience further obliges acute attention to climatic dimensions. Coastal vulnerability and the future of freshwater stocks are at risk from growing atmospheric disruption, manifest in saltwater inundation of aquifers and oscillations in precipitation. Proactive engineering and adaptive policy are indispensable if foundational infrastructure is to withstand the coming strain.

Urgency thus dictates alignment of development and economic policy, weaving resilience into the fabric of long-term growth calculation. Equally, contingency planning for external perturbations—be they distributed denial-of-service operations, regional military escalation, or rupture of international supply chains—diffuses the shock gradient. Within this strategic ensemble, resilience is transmuted into a normative civic obligation, valorising patient anticipatory engagement over reaction and division.

When regional states channel resources into long-term security, economic self-sufficiency, and environmentally sustainable policies, resilience shifts from a vague idea to a purposeful framework that propels collective regional advancement. In the Strait of Hormuz, where long-term stability is indispensable, concrete, confidence-building measures stand out as the necessary foundation. Dedicated formal communication mechanisms, whether through standing joint security committees or regular multilateral dialogue fora, can effectively curtail ambiguity, ease apprehensions, and shield vital shipping corridors from unintended escalation.

Deliberative multilateral structures should be representative, ensuring that the full spectrum of voices is represented. At the same time, equal attention must be accorded to the member states of the Gulf Cooperation Council, including the Sultanate of Oman and the Islamic Republic of Iran. Such inclusivity naturally predisposes partnerships to collaborative security ventures, ranging from synchronised maritime surveillance to real-time intelligence exchanges. These measures, conducted beneath a transparent and de-escalatory technical umbrella, offer greater safety without inviting corrosive arms races. To extend stability beyond exercises and operations, skilful diplomacy must address chronic grievances. Identifying negotiated mandates for scarce resource allocation, environmental conservation, and internationally agreed-upon shipping lanes can fortify a crisis-mitigation framework.

Neutral states, as well as impartial international organisations, can play an indispensable role as impartial facilitators. Their participation injects procedural confidence and reinforces a culture of openness. Concurrently, region-wide investments in commercial, governmental, and academic maritime technologies—such as satellite surveillance networks, AI-based pattern-of-life solutions, and resilient cyber infrastructures—offer a complementary defensive and economic line of resilience. The integration of these capabilities bestows the region with the agility to counter both naturally induced disruptions and intentionally orchestrated hostilities.

Nurturing indigenous technological industries does more than enhance economic autonomy; it also mitigates dependence on external partners, whose policies may intermittently strain regional cohesion. Nations of the Gulf region should embark on collaborative, multidisciplinary research initiatives aimed at customising advanced technologies to the peculiar climatic and morphological conditions of the peninsula. Vaccinating the development strategy against external shocks, parallel investment in renewables—particularly solar, due to its abundance—offers the dual advantage of ecological mitigation and the cultivation of enduring economic avenues.

Merging innovation with systematic regional partnerships establishes a self-reinforcing virtuous cycle, enhancing capabilities even as it cultivates mutual trust and confidence. When cooperating states enact observable and substantial dividends, the inclination to prolong coherence and duration in collaborative agendas amplifies. Sustaining such momentum requires the concurrent reinforcement of bilateral, trilateral, or multilateral diplomatic channels, as well as the internal consolidation of functional states embodied in transparent, accountable governance structures devoted to maintaining regional equilibrium. Progressively inseparable from the above is the development of autonomous security architecture, credibly founded upon indigenous workforce training, the establishment of robust logistics networks, and the crystallisation of self-reliance, such that the region, in the event of unanticipated shocks, depends on no external agency.

Public engagement is vital; by cultivating a shared sense of purpose within communities, a culture of cooperation and enduring patience is nurtured. This broader strategy enables states to pursue stability, independent of external dependencies or transient alliances. In the long term, the model institutionalises local ownership, reinforcing the premise that security is a shared enterprise, founded on authentic partnership, and perpetuated through the iterative enhancement of regional capabilities, knowledge, and talent.

References

Androjna, A., Brčko, T., Pavić, I., & Greidanus, H. (2020). Assessing cyber challenges of maritime navigation. *Journal of Marine Science and Engineering*, 8(10), 776. https://doi.org/10.3390/jmse8100776

Asia Karim, Manzoor Ahmad Naazer, Amna Mahmood, & Saiqa Bukhari. (2023). Maritime dimension of Modi's foreign policy: Indo-Gulf maritime cooperation and its implications for Pakistan. *Liberal Arts and Social Sciences International Journal (LASSIJ)*, 7, 202–220. https://doi.org/10.47264/idea.lassij/7.1.12

Aldawish, Abdulmalik Mohammed A. (2025). *The application of the transit passage regime in straits used for international navigation: A study of the Strait of Hormuz.* https://core.ac.uk/download/640799483.pdf

Astha Chadha. (2023). *Strategic rivalries in the Indo-Pacific.* Routledge eBooks. https://doi.org/10.4324/9781003336143-17

Berkofsky, A., & Sciorati, G. (2021). *Post-pandemic Asia.* https://core.ac.uk/download/478124715.pdf

Brewster, D. (2014). Beyond the 'string of pearls': Is there really a Sino-Indian security dilemma in the Indian Ocean?

Carter, C. M., Hood, J.-P., Jackson, M. J., Lonstein, et al. (2020). *Unmanned vehicle systems & operations on air, sea, land*. https://core.ac.uk/download/368330682.pdf

Croteau, S. (2025). *Securing the seas: The political economy of naval force structure*. https://core.ac.uk/download/650326500.pdf

D. J. B. Smith, Noah Bell, Jakob Faller, Victor Galaz, Albert V. Norström, Corey Pattison, & Cibele Queiroz. (2022). Elements of a planetary emergency: Environment of peace (Part 1). https://doi.org/10.55163/mdeb4357

Faculty of the Department of National Security Affairs, Naval Postgraduate School. (1998). *Summary of research 1998, Department of National Security Affairs*. https://core.ac.uk/download/36731602.pdf

Ferreira-Pereira, L. C., & Melo, D. S. N. de. (2022). The European Union and maritime security: Origins, developments and latest trends. https://core.ac.uk/download/561007826.pdf

Futter, A., Bracken, P., Castelli, L., Hunter, C., Samuel, O., Silvestri, F., & Zala, B. (2025). *The global third nuclear age*. https://doi.org/10.4324/9781003570707

Gábor András Papp. (2024). China's militarisation and the Indian Ocean. *Nemzet és Biztonság*, 16, 20–40. https://doi.org/10.32576/nb.2023.2.2

Habib Badawi. (2024). Chinese geoeconomics and geostrategic motives in a changing international order: Understanding the significance of a Chinese military base in Djibouti. *International Journal of Politics and Security*, 6, 67–99. https://doi.org/10.53451/ijps.1401481

Hao Wu, Syed Mehmood Ali Shah, Ahsan Nawaz, Ali Asad, Shahid Iqbal, Hafız Zahoor, & Ahsen Maqsoom. (2020). The impact of energy cooperation and the role of the One Belt and Road Initiative in revolutionizing the geopolitics of energy among regional economic powers: An analysis of infrastructure development and project management. *Complexity*, 2020, 1–16. https://doi.org/10.1155/2020/8820021

Hung Quoc Vo, Nguyễn Tuấn Bình, Hiep Tran, & T. P. Bui. (2023). US-China rivalry in Southeast Asia region: A study on the South China Sea case. *Journal of Liberty and International Affairs*, 9, 342–357. https://doi.org/10.47305/jlia2391342v

Isabela De Andrade Gama, Tutku Filiz, & Ljiljana Čabrilo Blagojević. (2021). [Title missing]. *Ukrainian Policymaker*, 8. https://doi.org/10.29202/up/8

Kelechukwu Dennis Ezeh, & Gerald E. Ezirim. (2023). Foreign military bases (FMBs) and economic security in Africa: Overview of FMBs in Djibouti. *International Journal of Geopolitics and Governance*, 2, 10–26. https://doi.org/10.37284/ijgg.2.1.1214

Kessler, G. C., & Zorri, D. M. (2021). Cross domain IW threats to SOF maritime missions: Implications for U.S. SOF. https://core.ac.uk/download/482044171.pdf

Kumara, J. S. (2021). *The sea power of small states: A case study of Sri Lanka*. https://core.ac.uk/download/493003648.pdf

Lortie, P. (2015). Asia-Pacific: A new agenda for the times ahead. https://core.ac.uk/download/151554006.pdf

Manfred Häfner, Pier Paolo Raimondi, & Benedetta Bonometti. (2023). *Geopolitics of oil and gas in the MENA region: Perspectives on development in the Middle East and North Africa (MENA) region*. https://doi.org/10.1007/978-3-031-30705-8_5

Md Syful Islam. (2024). Maritime security in a technological era: Addressing challenges in balancing technology and ethics. *Mersin University Journal of Maritime Faculty*, 6, 1–16.

https://doi.org/10.47512/meujmaf.1418239

O'Hara, M. P. (2016). *The navy as a political instrument: Freedom of navigation operations 1958–2013.* https://core.ac.uk/download/161453906.pdf

Ostrom, J. D. (2021). IRAN'S CHALLENGE TO THE U.S. IN THE MARITIME DOMAIN. https://core.ac.uk/download/483905719.pdf

Pugliese, G. (2022). The European Union's security intervention in the Indo-Pacific: Between multilateralism and mercantile interests. *Journal of Intervention and Statebuilding,* 17, 76–98. https://doi.org/10.1080/17502977.2022.2118425

Rykers, Y., Karlsrud, J., Brosig, M., Hofmann, S. C., Maglia, C., & Rieker, P. (2023). Ad hoc coalitions in global governance: Short-notice, task- and time-specific cooperation. *International Affairs,* 99(3), 727–745. https://doi.org/10.1093/ia/iiac319

Sahakyan, M. (2024). *Routledge handbook of Chinese and Eurasian international relations.* Routledge eBooks. https://doi.org/10.4324/9781003439110

Selth, A. (2022). Defence and national security. https://doi.org/10.1355/9789814951784-033

Shukri, S. (2025). Security community-building in the Mediterranean Sea: The roles of NATO and European Union in managing maritime challenges. https://core.ac.uk/download/444041195.pdf

Shaheen, M. (2025). *The Gwadar conundrum: Navigating the concerns and prospects of China's presence.* https://core.ac.uk/download/660899387.pdf

Song, Y.-M. (2023). Strategic reflection of Indian Ocean power duel between China and India around the Bay of Bengal. https://core.ac.uk/download/598494028.pdf

T. O. N., Miranda Priebe, Bryan Rooney, Nathan Beauchamp-Mustafaga, Jeffrey Martini, Stéphanie Pézard, G. John, et al. (2021). *Implementing restraint: Changes in U.S. regional security policies to operationalize a realist grand strategy of restraint*. RAND Corporation eBooks. https://doi.org/10.7249/rra739-1

V. Mikheev, & S. Lukonin. (2024). "Chinese coaster". *World Economy and International Relations*, 68(1), 19–30. https://doi.org/10.20542/0131-2227-2024-68-1-19-30

Wang, X., Wong, Y. D., Li, K. X., & Yuen, K. F. (2020). Transport research under Belt and Road Initiative: Current trends and future research agenda. *Transportmetrica A: Transport Science*, 17(4), 357–379. https://doi.org/10.1080/23249935.2020.1731008

Kupriyanov A.V. Russia and India: problems and prospects for cooperation. – Polis. Political Studies. 2022. No. 4. https://doi.org/10.17976/jpps/2022.04.06

www.ingramcontent.com/pod-product-compliance
Lightning Source LLC
Chambersburg PA
CBHW031152020426
42333CB00013B/629